# Getting Started with Tableau 2019.2
## *Second Edition*

Effective data visualization and business intelligence with the new features of Tableau 2019.2

**Tristan Guillevin**

BIRMINGHAM - MUMBAI

# Getting Started with Tableau 2019.2
## *Second Edition*

**Commissioning Editor**: Amey Varangaonkar
**Acquisition Editor:** Devika Battike
**Content Development Editor:** Unnati Guha
**Technical Editor:** Sayli Nikalje
**Copy Editor:** Safis Editing
**Project Coordinator:** Manthan Patel
**Proofreader:** Safis Editing
**Indexer:** Priyanka Dhadke
**Graphics:** Jisha Chirayil
**Production Designer:** Nilesh Mohite

First published: September 2018
Second edition: June 2019

Production reference: 1040619

Published by Packt Publishing Ltd.
Livery Place
35 Livery Street
Birmingham B3 2PB, UK.

ISBN 978-1-83855-306-7

www.packtpub.com

# Pack⟨t⟩

Packt.com

Subscribe to our online digital library for full access to over 7,000 books and videos, as well as industry leading tools to help you plan your personal development and advance your career. For more information, please visit our website.

## Why subscribe?

- Spend less time learning and more time coding with practical eBooks and Videos from over 4,000 industry professionals

- Learn better with Skill Plans built especially for you

- Get a free eBook or video every month

- Fully searchable for easy access to vital information

- Copy and paste, print, and bookmark content

Did you know that Packt offers eBook versions of every book published, with PDF and ePub files available? You can upgrade to the eBook version at www.Packt.com and as a print book customer, you are entitled to a discount on the eBook copy. Get in touch with us at customercare@packtpub.com for more details.

At www.Packt.com, you can also read a collection of free technical articles, sign up for a range of free newsletters, and receive exclusive discounts and offers on Packt books and eBooks.

# Contributors

## About the author

**Tristan Guillevin** started his professional life in 2015 as a consultant, where he discovered Tableau. Quickly, data visualization became a real passion! During this time, he provided data visualization expertise to more than thirty clients in many different sectors around the world. In 2017, Tristan won the global Iron Viz competition in Las Vegas. Now, he helps people with Tableau through webinars, conferences, blog articles, and this book! Tristan currently works at Ogury as a data visualization engineer.

I'd like to first thank Laura for her daily support and understanding. Writing a book is not an easy task, even for a second edition. A special thanks to Ivett, Sayli, Unnati, and all the Packt team for making the publication of this book possible. Finally, to everyone with the same passion for data visualization, thanks for having contributed making this passion grow on me, from my first bar chart to the completion of this book.

# About the reviewer

**Ivett Kovács** was always very comfortable with data—after majoring in statistics, she started working as a data analyst. She was one of the first Hungarian power users of Tableau Desktop 2012, and has been mastering Tableau ever since. Currently, she is Starschema's senior data visualization expert, leading a team of 10+ dataviz developers. She is not only Tableau certified, but has also been a Tableau Ambassador since 2017, as well as an Iron Viz judge.

She is also a featured volunteer with Viz for Social Good. She has developed several Tableau dashboards on various social topics, such as the refugee crisis and gender inequality in tech companies and political institutions.

# Packt is searching for authors like you

If you're interested in becoming an author for Packt, please visit `authors.packtpub.com` and apply today. We have worked with thousands of developers and tech professionals, just like you, to help them share their insight with the global tech community. You can make a general application, apply for a specific hot topic that we are recruiting an author for, or submit your own idea.

# Table of Contents

# Preface

Tableau is one of the leading data visualization tools and is regularly updated with new functionalities and features. The latest release, Tableau 2019.2 promises new and advanced features related to visual analytics, reporting, dashboarding, and a host of other data visualization aspects. *Getting Started with Tableau 2019.2* will get you up to speed with these additional functionalities.

The book starts by highlighting the new functionalities of Tableau 2019.2 providing concrete examples of how to use them. However, if you're new to Tableau, don't worry—you'll be guided through the major aspects of Tableau with relevant examples. You'll learn how to connect to data, build a data source, visualize your data, build a Dashboard, and even share data online. In the concluding chapters, you'll delve into advanced techniques, such as creating a cross-database join and data blending.

By the end of this book, you'll be able to use Tableau effectively to create quick, cost-effective, and business-efficient **business intelligence (BI)** solutions.

# Who this book is for

Existing Tableau users and BI professionals who want to get up to speed with what's new in Tableau 2019 will find this beginner-level book to be a very useful resource. No, you can start without any experience. This is a book for beginner. They can start with absolutely no knowledge.

# What this book covers

*Chapter 1, Catching Up with Tableau 2019,* explains every new feature of the different Tableau 2019 versions. You'll learn how to use them with clear explanations, examples, and tutorials. This chapter is the best way to catch up with the new releases if you already have some Tableau knowledge. Beginners should start with *Chapter 2, The Tableau Core.*

*Chapter 2, The Tableau Core,* explains the basics that every Tableau users should know. It contains an overview of the different products, a description of Tableau's workspaces, wordings, and clear explanations of Tableau's most crucial concepts, such as Dimension, Measure, Discrete, Continuous, Live, and Extract.

*Chapter 3, Getting Started with Tableau Desktop,* represents your first real experience with Tableau and is designed as a guided tutorial. In just one chapter you'll connect to data, build three visualizations, an interactive dashboard, and answer business questions with the power of Tableau's data exploration capabilities.

*Chapter 4, Connecting to Data and Simple Transformations,* focuses on data connections, starting with general rules when connecting to files and servers. This chapter also goes into detail about essential features such as Joins, Unions, and Transformations (Pivot, Split, and more).

*Chapter 5, Building an Efficient Data Source,* helps you build the best data source for your analysis. Having a customized and well-organized data source is crucial in Tableau. You'll learn the different elements that compose a data source, how to refresh and deals with the changes, and change the default format. This chapter also focuses on creating Groups, Hierarchies, Sets, and Bins.

*Chapter 6, Design Insightful Visualizations,* teaches you the different ways of building visualizations in Tableau with double-clicks, the Show Me menu, or simple drag and drops. You'll also see a description of the different Mark Types and properties. Then you will learn how to build visualizations with multiple measures thanks to Dual Axis, or Measure Name and Measure Values. Filters, Quick-Filters, Pages, and an overview of the different options available complete the global vision of what you can do when creating a visualization.

*Chapter 7, Powerful Dashboards, Stories, and Actions,* is a key chapter in which you'll learn the basics about building dashboards in Tableau with an overview of the different objects available and advice about which layout to use. You'll also see how to add interactivity with the different Actions, and how to tell compelling stories with the Story points.

*Chapter 8, Publishing and Interacting in Tableau Server,* is the culmination of what you've learned in the previous chapters. This chapter focuses on Tableau Server/Online, how to publish your dashboards and Data Sources online, how to interact with published content, and how to build device-specific layouts.

*Chapter 9, An Introduction to Calculations,* is the first advanced chapter where you'll expand Tableau's capabilities by creating new calculated fields with powerful formulas. After describing the basics of calculation, you'll understand how to use advanced formulas such as Table Calculation and Level Of Detail.

*Chapter 10, Analytics and Parameters,* focuses on two significant aspects of Tableau that combine well. The first part, Analytics, describes how to add Reference Lines, Forecast, Clusters, Trend Lines, Totals, and more. The second part explains how to create and use parameters to add more interactivity to your analysis. Finally, you'll create a real-life business usage combining analytics features, parameters, and calculations.

*Chapter 11, Advanced Data Connections,* presents three major features: cross-database Join and data-blending to create analyses that combine multiple connection types, and Wildcard Unions to build automatic unions based on multiple files. This chapter will help you tackle data connection challenges.

*Chapter 12, Dealing with Security,* is the last technical chapter of this book and focuses on three ways to secure your data: permissions on Tableau Server, user filters on Tableau Desktop, and row-level data security in your data.

*Chapter 13, How to Keep Growing Your Skills,* is a non-technical but essential chapter. You'll discover many ways of learning new things and growing your Tableau skills thanks to community projects. The chapter is also a tribute to the Tableau community, presenting many ways to be part of that big family, which shares a passion for data visualization with Tableau.

# To get the most out of this book

No prerequisites are necessary. Tableau is designed to be simple to use for everyone, no matter their background. This book starts from the very beginning and will teach you all major concepts.

# Download the example code files

You can download the example code files for this book from your account at
`http://www.packt.com`. If you purchased this book elsewhere, you can visit
`http://www.packt.com/support` and register to have the files emailed directly
to you.

You can download the code files by following these steps:

1. Log in or register at `http://www.packt.com`.
2. Select the **SUPPORT** tab.
3. Click on **Code Downloads & Errata**.
4. Enter the name of the book in the **Search** box and follow the on-screen instructions.

Once the file is downloaded, please make sure that you unzip or extract the folder
using the latest version of:

- WinRAR / 7-Zip for Windows
- Zipeg / iZip / UnRarX for Mac
- 7-Zip / PeaZip for Linux

The code bundle for the book is also hosted on GitHub at: `https://github.com/
PacktPublishing/Getting-Started-with-Tableau-2019.2`. In case there's an
update to the code, it will be updated on the existing GitHub repository.

We also have other code bundles from our rich catalog of books and videos available
at `https://github.com/PacktPublishing/`. Check them out!

# Download the color images

We also provide a PDF file that has color images of the screenshots/diagrams
used in this book. You can download it here: `http://www.packtpub.com/sites/
default/files/downloads/9781838553067 _ColorImages.pdf`.

# Conventions used

There are a number of text conventions used throughout this book.

`CodeInText`: Indicates code words in text, database table names, folder names,
filenames, file extensions, pathnames, dummy URLs, user input, and Twitter
handles. For example: "When you open Tableau Desktop, you start working on a
Workbook. After you're done working, you save your work in a `.twb` or `.twbx` file."

**Bold**: Indicates a new term, an important word, or words that you see on the screen, for example, in menus or dialog boxes, also appear in the text like this. For example: "Double-click on **Order date**. Tableau automatically transforms the bar into a line."

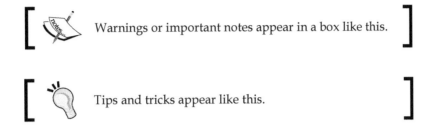

Warnings or important notes appear in a box like this.

Tips and tricks appear like this.

# Get in touch

Feedback from our readers is always welcome.

**General feedback**: If you have questions about any aspect of this book, mention the book title in the subject of your message and email us at customercare@packtpub.com.

**Errata**: Although we have taken every care to ensure the accuracy of our content, mistakes do happen. If you have found a mistake in this book we would be grateful if you would report this to us. Please visit, http://www.packt.com/submit-errata, selecting your book, clicking on the Errata Submission Form link, and entering the details.

**Piracy**: If you come across any illegal copies of our works in any form on the internet, we would be grateful if you would provide us with the location address or website name. Please contact us at copyright@packt.com with a link to the material.

**If you are interested in becoming an author**: If there is a topic that you have expertise in and you are interested in either writing or contributing to a book, please visit http://authors.packtpub.com.

# Reviews

Please leave a review. Once you have read and used this book, why not leave a review on the site that you purchased it from? Potential readers can then see and use your unbiased opinion to make purchase decisions, we at Packt can understand what you think about our products, and our authors can see your feedback on their book. Thank you!

For more information about Packt, please visit packt.com.

# Section 1: An Introduction to Tableau

This section will cover the basics of Tableau and will give you a heads up on the new features of Tableau 2019. We will take a look at different Tableau products, such as Tableau Desktop and Tableau Server. We will describe the Tableau lexicon so that all the terms of Tableau that will feature in this book can be understood. We'll also learn about different workplaces to explain how the interface works and understand the toolbars.

This section will include the following chapters:

- *Chapter 1, Catching Up with Tableau 2019*
- *Chapter 2, The Tableau Core*
- *Chapter 3, A First Dashboard and Exploration*

# 1
# Catching Up with Tableau 2019

Thank you for purchasing *Getting Started with Tableau 2019.2*. As its title suggests, this book aims to provide you with explanations, advice, tips, and the best practices to start (or continue) your journey through Tableau using the most recent features. You'll always find clear descriptions, reproducible examples, and tutorials. Whether you already know how to use Tableau and want to get familiar with its latest features, or you've never used the tool and want to learn from the beginning, this book is for you, and I hope you enjoy it.

If you are a Tableau user looking for information about its new features and how to use them, you are in the right place. If you are new to Tableau, start with *Chapter 2, The Tableau Core,* to learn about the basics and advanced features of Tableau. Throughout this book, many new features will be explained. Having finished all of the chapters, you can come back here to learn about the newest features in detail.

In this first chapter, we'll cover the new features in Tableau's 2019 releases (2019.1 and 2019.2). This chapter will be divided into two parts, as follows:

- Connector improvements
- Worksheet enhancement
- New actions
- Empowered Dashboard
- Tableau Server

For each part, each major feature has its own section. Next to the name of the feature, between brackets, the version that introduced the new feature will be specified.

This book focuses on data visualization with Tableau Desktop and Tableau Server/Online. Tableau Prep is not covered, as it fulfills a different need. You can learn more about Tableau Prep at https://www.tableau.com/products/prep.

Let's start with Tableau Desktop; get ready to discover many great new features!

To understand and reproduce the examples provided in this chapter, you need to know how to connect to data, build a data source, and create Worksheets and Dashboards.

# Connector improvements

There are no changes regarding the way you connect to data or what you can do with data sources. However, the newest version of Tableau includes four new connectors, all of which have been available since Tableau 2019.1:

- Azure SQL Data Warehouse Connector
- Google Ads Connector
- Google Drive
- MariaDB

Some other data source improvements are as follows:

- OAuth is enabled for a Snowflake connector (2019.1)
- You can directly use the power of spatial information in a PostgreSQL+PostGIS database without having to export or prep the data (2019.1)
- The JDBC connector was improved for better performance (2019.2)
- You can connect to on-premise Service Now deployments (2019.2)
- You can use Azure Active Directory username and password authentication (2019.2)
- Enhanced SAP Hana and Marketo connectors (2019.2)

Now, let's take a look at visualization improvements.

# Worksheet enhancement

Mapping is the star of the newest Tableau version. We'll cover the new `MakePoint` and `MakeLine` functions, as well as the new vector map. These two new features will allow you to enjoy building maps even more than before.

# MakePoint and MakeLine (2019.2)

Since Tableau 10.2, you have been able to connect to a spatial file to create maps using the Geometry field (a Point, a Line, or a Polygon). Each new release brought new capabilities, such as using a spatial field directly from a database or the recent spatial join: **Intersect**. Tableau Desktop 2019.2 brings two new functionalities: MakePoint and MakeLine.

MakePoint and MakeLine are two new functions. MakePoint converts Latitude and Longitude into a spatial point. MakeLine takes two Points and creates a spatial Line. This allows you to create a path between two places on Earth by taking into account the curvature of the earth and joining spatial and nonspatial files with Latitude and Longitude.

Let's visualize the top 100 busiest air routes.

 Download the `Flights.xlsx` Excel file from the **Chapter 1: Catching up with Tableau 2019** section of my website, `https://tableau2019.ladataviz.com` or browse to `https://ladataviz.com/wp-content/uploads/2019/05/Flights.xlsx`.

This file contains one hundred lines and provides information on the departure and arrival to airports, as well as the number of passengers.

Let's start:

1. Open Tableau Desktop and select **Microsoft Excel**.
2. Connect to the `Flights.xlsx` file you've just downloaded.
3. On Sheet1, create a new calculated field. Name it `Departure Point` and write the following formula: `MAKEPOINT([Departure Latitude],[Departure Longitude])`.
4. Create a second calculated field for the arrivals. Name it `Arrival Point` and write the following formula: `MAKEPOINT([Arrival Latitude], [Arrival Longitude])`.
5. You have created two calculated fields that contain spatial points that are mapping the departure and arrival airports. You can test your fields by simply double-clicking on them.
6. Create a final calculated field for the routes. Name it `Air Routes` and write the following formula: `MAKELINE([Departure Point],[Arrival Point])`.
7. On a blank Worksheet, double-click on Air Routes; this will automatically generate all the paths on a map.

8. To finalize the visualization, add the **Route** Dimension in **Detail** to separate each path, and add the **Passengers** Measure in **Size** and **Color** to visually spot the busiest routes. The following screenshot shows the final results:

If, like me, you aren't new to Tableau, you will be impressed by how fast and easy it is to achieve this now. That's what we love about each new Tableau release: it always makes our analysis faster and easier to do.

As I said, mapping is the star, so let's continue with this new mapping style.

# Vector Map (2019.2)

Are you ready for a smoother, faster, and more powerful than ever mapping experience? Yes, you are! Using maps in Tableau Desktop 2019.2 never felt better. Using the MapBox technology, Tableau maps now use vectors for an incredibly smooth zoom in and out.

Go ahead – open your favorite visualization that includes a map and try it yourself!

But that's not all! Let's open the **Maps Layers** pane using the **Map** top menu. Three new styles have been added. You can now visualize your data using the **Streets**, **Outdoors**, or **Satellite** styles. I can now show you where I grew up; *good luck finding it*:

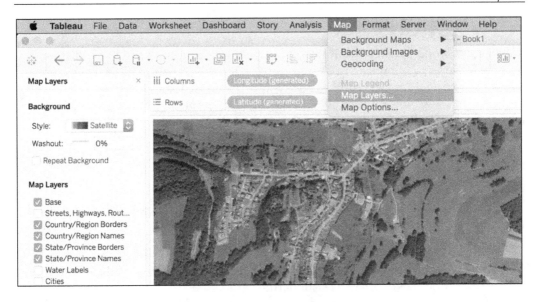

Oh! And is if this wasn't enough, there are also new data layers that you can add: **Terrain**, **Routes**, **Water Labels**, **Cities**, **Point of Interest**, **Neighborhoods**, **Building Footprints**, and so on. Each style has newer and richer layers. Mapping has never been so good.

# Other improvements

The following is a list of other small visualization improvements:

- **Sort Controls**: On the Worksheet top menu, you'll find a new option, **Show Sort Controls,** which allows you to choose whether users can change the sort order. (2019.2)

- **Nested sort**: You can now use the nested sort feature on multiple dimensions (2019.1)

- **Tooltip reference line**: On the reference line configuration window, you can now modify and even totally remove the tooltip (2019.2)

Now, we'll look at the new features available for Dashboards.

# New actions

Tableau's power resides in the ability to build simple and powerful visualizations and dashboards in minutes, but also to create interactivity with only a few clicks thanks to Actions. Tableau 2018.3 already introduced two new actions: *Go To Sheet* and *Change Set Values*. Tableau 2019.1 and 2019.2 continue to improve on these actions with a great enhancement for *Go to URL* actions and a revolutionary way of working with parameters: *Change Parameter*.

## Improved URL Actions (2019.1)

The **Go to URL...** action allows you to open a website directly inside the Dashboard or in a new window. With effect from version 2019.2, you have the ability to choose how to open the URL target in the configuration window:

- **New Browser tab**: Always opens the link in a new browser tab, even if a Web Page object exists in the Dashboard.
- **Web Page object**: Opens the URL in a Web Page object in your Dashboard. You can even have multiple Web Page objects in your Dashboard with multiple URL actions targeting each Web Page object separately.
- **Browser tab if no Web Page objects exists**: The default option; this opens the URL in a browser tab if there is no Web Page object.

Let's continue with *Change Parameters*.

## Change Parameter (2019.2)

The Change Parameter... is the newest action to be introduced in Tableau 2019.2. It allows you to change the value of a Parameter based on the value on a Worksheet. It was already possible to achieve this thanks to Extensions, but now Tableau has made it official!

Previously, modifying the value of a Parameter was only possible using the Parameter Control card. Now, you can use any action triggers (**Hover**, **Select**, or **Menu**) to modify the current value of a Parameter. As for the highlight action, the value you want to pass to the Parameter has to be in the View.

Let's create an example together. We want to compare the sales value of a state to a parameter and see if the sales are above or below the Parameter's value. The value of the Parameter will be automatically set when you hover over a state, allowing you to easily compare a state with others. For this example, you can use the `Sample - Superstore` saved data source. Perform the following steps:

1. On a blank Worksheet, create a new Parameter.

2. On the Parameter configuration window, name it `Sales` comparison value, of the Float type with **All allowable values**, and then click on **OK**. Your Parameter configuration should look like this:

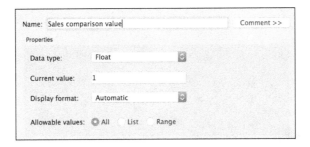

3. Create a new calculated field, name it `Sales comparison`, and write the following formula: `SUM([Sales])-[Sales comparison value]`.

4. Double-click on **State**, then put **Sales** in **Detail** and **Sales Comparison** in **Color**. Your visualization should look like this:

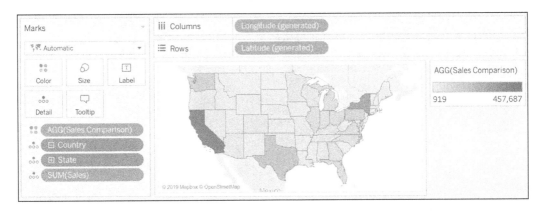

5. Open the **Worksheet** top menu and click on **Actions...**.

6. Click on the **Add Action** button and choose **Change Parameter...**.

7. Name the action `Set sales comparison value` and set it to run on
**Hover**. In the **Target Parameter** list, choose **Sales comparison value**, and
in the **Value** list, choose **SUM(Sales)**. Keep the **Aggregation** as **Sum**. Your
configuration window should look as follows:

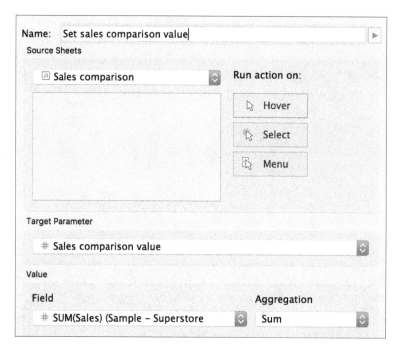

8. Back in your visualization, hovering over a state should change the value
of the parameter and therefore allow you to quickly compare the sales of
a state to the others. The following is the final result when you hover over
Washington:

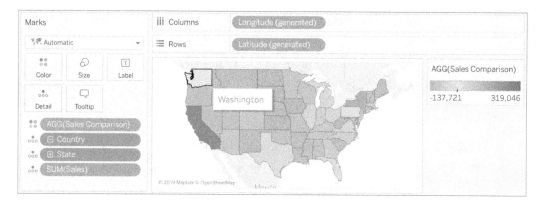

This new action will unlock many new opportunities so that you can create awesome interactions for your users. I can't wait to see what the Tableau Community will create!

Let's continue with all the new features of the Dashboard.

# Empowered Dashboard

Building Dashboards is definitely one of the most important aspects of using Tableau Desktop. Fortunately, building a simple Dashboard is also something very easy and enjoyable to do. In the process of always making our life easier, Tableau has developed a few very nice new features.

The first important new feature is the ability to show or hide a container with a totally new button.

# Show/Hide containers (2019.2)

If you are not new to Tableau, I'm sure you've already made *(or had to make)* a Dashboard with lots of filters and legends. You know, something that looks like this:

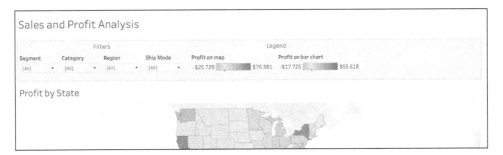

Rejoice, because this is over! You can now add a toggle button to containers, allowing you and your user to show or hide it at will. There's only one condition at the moment, which is that the container needs to be floating.

Adding a toggle button is quite easy: select the containers (with the **Select Container** option when you click on an item, or use the **Item hierarchy** in the **Layout** pane), then select **Add toggle button** from the container options. A default toggle button is automatically added to your Dashboard. Among the button options, you'll find the ability to **Show** or **Hide** the container and edit it with the **Edit Button...** option.

You can also use the *Alt + Click* shortcut to perform the button action. Of course, this is only needed in editor mode. When the Dashboard is published or open with Tableau Reader, the button is triggered by a simple click.

If you click on **Edit Button...** a new window will open. Here, you can choose what Dashboard element will be impacted by the button, the **Button Style** (image or text), and the **Button Appearance**. The Button Appearance part lets you choose the **Image** (or Title and Font), **Border**, **Background**, and **Tooltip** when the item is currently shown or hidden.

Let's create an example together. We will use this new feature to enhance the example that was provided at the beginning of this section.

 Download the ZIP file named `ToggleButtonStart.zip` from the **Chapter 1: Catching up with Tableau 2019** section of my website, `https://tableau2019.ladataviz.com` or, browse to `https://ladataviz.com/wp-content/uploads/2019/05/ToggleButtonStart.zip`.

Unzip the `ToggleButtonStart.zip` file and you'll find a Tableau Packaged Workbook that is the start of the example:

1. Open the `ToggleButtonStart.twbx` workbook.

2. Select the filters and legend container, either by double-clicking on the grip part or using the **Select Containers** option of the items, or by using the **Item hierarchy** in the **Layout** pane. You should see the entire horizontal container with a blue outline, like this:

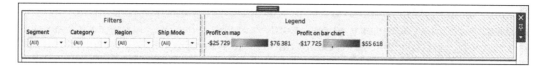

3. Go to the option using the descending arrow and select **Floating**.

4. Using the grip part, move the containers at the top left. Then, by selecting the left border, increase its width, as shown in the following screenshot:

5. Click on the arrow to option the container options and select **Add Show/ Hide** button.

6. You can now use this button to show and hide the container with the filters and legends. To finalize the Dashboard, you can move the button next to the title, increase its size, and add a tooltip among the button options. Here's the final result:

This new feature allows everyone to build clearer and more efficient Dashboards. The next feature is really simple to understand and use, but will definitely help you save a lot of time.

# Replace Worksheets (2019.2)

This is the kind of feature we love: simple and efficient. With Tableau 2019.2, you can now replace any Worksheet in a Dashboard with another new Worksheet. This may not sound like a big deal to newcomers, but Tableau veterans know how useful this new feature is.

To replace a Worksheet, select the existing Worksheet in the Dashboard. Then, on the **Sheets** pane on the left, hover over the replacement Worksheet and click on the button highlighted in the following screenshot:

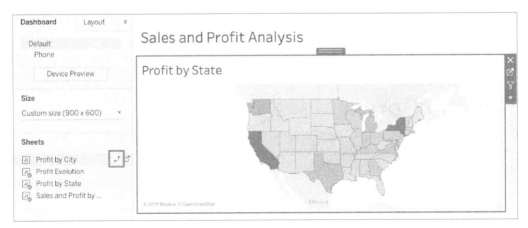

That's it! Again: simple and efficient.

Let's finish with the other improvements.

# Other improvements

Don't think that the next three improvements don't have their own sections because they aren't important! I decided to group them only because they are all really easy to explain, understand, and use, as you will discover:

- **Export to PowerPoint**: On Tableau Desktop, among the **File** top menu, you'll find the **Export As PowerPoint** option. On Tableau Server, you'll find the PowerPoint option when you click on the **Download** button in the toolbar. In Tableau 2019.2, this feature was improved to export Stories, with each Story point being a new slide (2019.1).

- **Name zone**: In the **Item hierarchy** part of the **Layout** pane of a Dashboard, you can now give a meaningful name to each item. This is a great feature to combine with the Show/Hide button. Here's an example (2019.1):

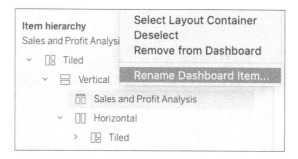

- **Auto phone layout**: Any Dashboard built with Tableau Desktop 2019.1 or later automatically starts with an automatically generated phone layout. Don't forget to remove it if you don't want it (2019.1).

That's it for Tableau Desktop. In the next section, we'll see what's new in Tableau Server.

# Tableau Server

Ask Data is without a doubt one of the most important new features of the 2019 releases. However, the change that everyone will directly spot is the totally new browsing experience, with a new way to group published content and a fresh look.

# New browsing experience (2019.2)

Tableau Server 2019.1 introduced Mixed Content. This new way of grouping content mixes data sources, Workbooks, flows, and sub-projects in the same view of a project. Say goodbye to different tabs for each content type. Now, you can see everything at the same time. For example, here's the view of a project, **World Indicators**, that contains a sub-project, Workbooks, and a data source:

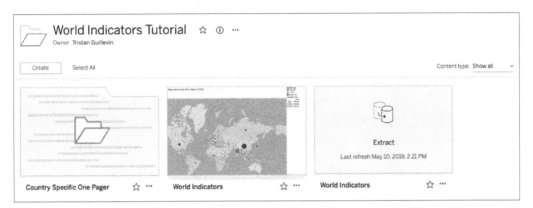

Tableau Server 2019.2 pushes this change further with a totally new look and feel when navigating on Tableau Server. The new **Home** page displays your recently used content, your favorites, and what other Tableau users are viewing. The top menu has also totally disappeared to leave room for a new left navigation pane. Don't be afraid – the options are still the same. Here's the new **Home** page:

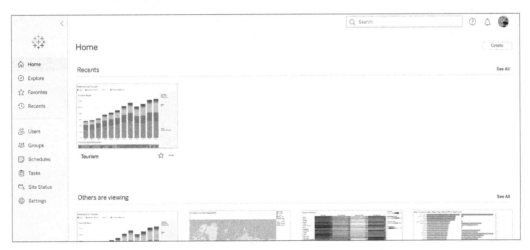

As you may have noticed, if you click on a data source, a strange and new tab will open. I said strange, but I should have used the word awesome. This is Ask Data.

# Ask Data (2019.1)

Ask Data is the first view that opens when you click on a data source. It's a new tool to query any data sources using the English language. With this new feature, Tableau Server becomes more and more easy to use for everyone. But how does it work, exactly?

On the left, you'll find something similar to the Data pane in Tableau Desktop, and in the middle, a simple search bar with some suggestions. The following is an example of **Ask Data** when using the Sample - Superstore data source:

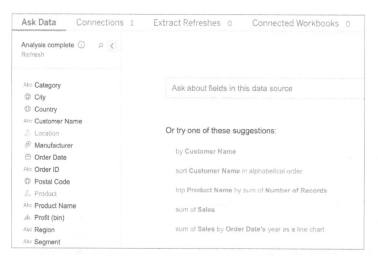

All you have to do is ask. Write something in the search bar and a new browser tab will automatically open with the result of what you asked for. For example, if you write sum of profit by state, Ask Data automatically creates a map with the sales in color:

Without any knowledge of how to use Tableau to create a visualization, Ask Data was able to convert some text into a visualization.

On the **Data** pane on the left, when you hover over a field, a nice tooltip gives you some quick insights about the number of values, their distribution, and even the formula (if it's a calculated field). But wait—there's more! If you click on the small arrow next to a field, you can use the **Edit synonyms** option. When you add a synonym to a field, you are able to use that synonym in your sentence to create the visualization.

On the top, you can see that the search bar has expanded and suggested that you can adjust the question or use the **Clear All** button to start over. Here are some examples of what you can add:

- **as a bar chart**, changes the viz type to a bar (works with different Marks type)
- **by category**, adds the category in the View
- **in December 2018** filters the order date
- With effect from 2019.2, you can also use **replace profit with sales, add sales,** or **remove profit** , which do exactly what they say

 Next to the visualization, you can also use the selector to change the Marks type.

If you are satisfied with the visualization but you want to quickly change a Measure or Dimension, you can click on different fields in the query box to open a menu that allows you to choose a different field and its aggregation. For example, if you click on **sum of Profit**, you can quickly change it to display the discount instead, as you can see in the following screenshot:

The 2019.2 version of Tableau Server pushes Ask Data even further, allowing you to write simple calculations such as `avg sales / avg profit`, but you can also create multiple Sheets and save the workbook directly in a project.

Of course, Ask Data doesn't have the flexibility of Tableau Desktop, and you don't have much control over what the result will be. However, it can easily supply a feature users have long demanded: *Can you just build a big table where I can search what I want?*. With Ask Data, you don't need that anymore.

Next, we'll look at a nice evolution for the alerts.

# New Alerts view (2019.2)

Alerts is an amazing feature that you can use to receive emails when your data satisfies a condition. With Tableau Server 2019.2, clicking on the Alerts button in the toolbar doesn't open the alert creation window anymore; instead, it opens a new pane on the right. Here's the **Alerts** view:

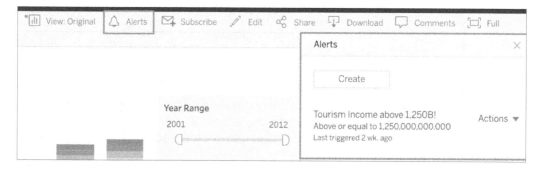

Thanks to this new pane, you can create alerts using the **Create** button, but also view and subscribe to all the existing Alerts that have been set by other users. When you click on an Alert, you will see all of its details (condition, last triggered, owner, and so on).

With effect from Tableau 2019.1, every Dashboard has a phone layout by default. Its new features will help you preview it.

# Device preview (2019.1)

With effect from Tableau 2019.1, you can preview the layouts on Tableau Server. Above the toolbar, a new button, **Preview Device Layouts**, is now available, as highlighted in the following screenshot:

When you click on the button, Tableau opens preview mode, where you can select **Laptop**, **Tablet**, or **Phone** to see how your Dashboard renders on those different devices.

Let's finish this section with a few other improvements.

# Other improvements

Here is a list of other new features available on Tableau Server:

- **New connections**: You can connect to Google Big Query, Google Drive, Dropbox, and OneDrive from the web (2019.1)

- **Okta improvement**: Tableau Server can integrate Okta identity management for users, groups, and roles even better (2019.1)

- **Site Start page**: Tableau Server admins can set a start page for all users (2019.2)

- **Create Parameters**: You can create Parameters in web editor mode (2019.2)

- Custom view for Viewer: A Viewer role user can now create custom views (2019.2)

- **Secure Rserve and TabPy connections**: You can host Rserve (2019.1) and TabPy (2019.2) servers remotely from Tableau Server and secure data in transit

# Summary

We are in the middle of the year, and with only two new releases, Tableau has already considerably improved its products.

Your Tableau life is now easier than ever before. You can add buttons to show and hide containers, automatically replace a Worksheet in a Dashboard, customize the reference line tooltip, show the sorts control, name your Dashboard zone, control the URL action targets, and sort without having to think twice.

You can also do more than ever. With the new Parameter actions, you will be able to create new types of interactivity between data and users. With the awesome vector maps and new spatial calculations, working with maps has never felt so good.

Ask Data is also a breaking change of Tableau Server for those of you who are already building worksheets and dashboards with Tableau Desktop, but also to all the potential users within your company. They don't need to learn Tableau to build insights. They don't have to understand what a dimension is, nor a measure or how to filter. All they have to do is ask.

2019 is already a great year for Tableau users and the Tableau community. This first chapter, which described its new features, is now over. If you learned how to use Tableau with this book, I hope that this chapter has provided you with a greater desire to use Tableau. If you already know Tableau, I hope this chapter gives you a clear idea and the motivation to use the new versions that are available.. Also, I'm sure this book has more to teach you (and that's surely why you purchased it), so don't hesitate to continue reading: read the tips, try the tutorials, and learn more about Tableau Desktop, Tableau Server, and the Tableau community.

# 2

# The Tableau Core

New to Tableau? You are in the right place to start! Tableau is simple, and you could start using it without any training. However, using it the wrong way, or without knowing the basics, is a big mistake. I have met many people who were unhappy with Tableau, just because they never learned the basics.

To begin, we'll go through all the things that every Tableau user should know. The following topics will be covered in this chapter:

- The different Tableau products
- Speaking Tableau
- Dimensions and Measures
- Blue and green – Discrete and Continuous
- The toolbar options
- Live or Extract

By the end of this chapter, you'll have all the knowledge you need to start your Tableau journey in the best possible way.

## The different Tableau products

There are seven Tableau products:

- **Tableau Desktop** is software that you can install on your computer. It is the core tool to connect to the data, build a data source, and create visualizations and Dashboards.
- **Tableau Server** is an online tool for sharing your work in a business environment. You need this tool to secure your data. Tableau Server is accessible with a simple browser. Your company hosts the server where Tableau server is installed.

- **Tableau Online** is the same as Tableau Server, but hosted by Tableau. They do the updates and maintenance, but you lose some personalization features.

- **Tableau Reader** is software that you can install on your computer that can read Tableau Desktop files. With Tableau Reader, you are not able to modify the Workbooks, but you can open them and keep all the interactivity, making it better than a PDF export or a picture.

- **Tableau Public** is free software with almost the same capabilities as Tableau Desktop, but you can only save your work online in a public environment, and not all connectors are available. Of course, it's not the best option if you don't want to share your data with the world, but it's a great place to find inspiration and share public visualizations.

- **Tableau Mobile** is an application that you can install on your smartphone or tablet. You can connect to a server and visualize your Dashboard directly with the app.

- **Tableau Prep** is a new software that is very different from the others. It is not a data visualization tool, but a data preparation tool. We'll not discuss Tableau Prep in this book. However, be aware that it exists, and it is a great solution for cleaning and preparing your data.

Like every tool, Tableau has its wording. Let's now learn how to speak Tableau.

# Speaking Tableau

Rather than a big list of all the terms, let's go through the basic Tableau life cycle.

When you open Tableau Desktop, you start working on a Workbook. After you've finished working, you will save your work in a .twb or .twbx file. You can open multiple instances of Tableau, each of them being a different Workbook.

The first page you see when you open Tableau Desktop is the Start page. Here, you can connect to data, open recent workbooks, discover the Viz of the Week, and open your saved data sources quickly.

After choosing your connector (a **Comma Separated Values (CSV)** file, an Excel file, or a database on a server), Tableau opens the data source workplace. On this page, you create the data source by choosing tables (or sheets) and creating joins, unions, or other transformations. The following screenshot illustrates the **Data Source** workplace:

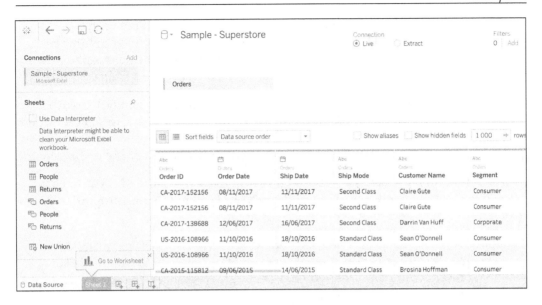

When you're done with the Data Source, you can start building a visualization in a Worksheet. **Sheet 1** is your first Worksheet. Here's the Worksheet workplace:

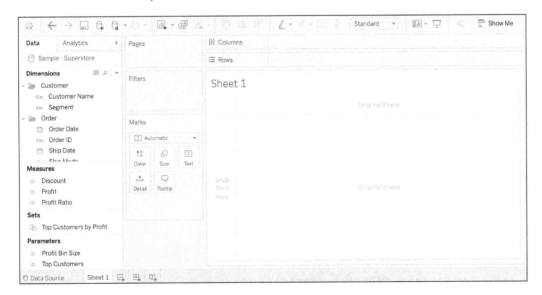

On the left, you can see your Data Source with all the fields split between two elements: **Measures** and **Dimensions**. Each field has a data type (**Text**, **Number**, **Boolean**, and so on). Later, you'll learn how to create new fields or elements, such as Groups, Bins, Hierarchies, Sets, Parameters, or Calculated Fields.

The big blank part is the **View**. It is here that your visualization will be displayed. Around the View, you can see different shelves (**Rows**, **Columns**, **Pages**, **Filters**, and **Marks**). To create visualizations, you have to put fields on those shelves. Once a field is on a shelf, it is called a **pill**. Pills can be green if **Continuous,** or blue if **Discrete**.

In the View, every distinct element you can select (click on) is called a **Mark**. Each Mark has one type (Bar, Circle, Line, and so on) and can have some properties (Color, Size, Label, and so on).

In Tableau, one Worksheet is one idea, one way of answering a question, and one visualization. You can create as many Worksheets as you want to find the best way to represent your data. Once you have enough Worksheets to answer all your questions, you can create a Dashboard.

A Dashboard is a combination of multiple Worksheets and objects (Containers, Image, Extensions, and so on). You can use actions to add interactivity between the different Worksheets.

If you want to tell a Story with your data, you can create a Story. The goal of the Story is to prepare a succession of **Story points** (each of them could be a Dashboard or a Worksheet). Each Story point is a new insight into your Story where you can customize the filters and captions and add some text. When presenting or sharing a Story, every interaction or explanation is already done.

After all of that, you can **publish** your Dashboard and Stories by using **Tableau Server/Online** or **Tableau Public** Voilà, you're done!

A bit overwhelmed? Don't worry, each chapter of this book focuses on a specific part of Tableau, and you'll have plenty of time to get familiar with these words with real examples. However, two words do require more in-depth explanations: Dimension and Measure.

# Dimension and Measure

When you create a data source, the fields are split between Dimensions and Measures. The Measure is what you want to analyze, and the Dimension is the angle of analysis.

By default, numbers are Measures, and the other data types (Text, String, Date, Geographical Boolean) are Dimensions, However, that's not always the case. Any data type can potentially be either a Dimension or a Measure.

A Dimension contains qualitative information. It always splits the number of Marks and is never aggregated.

A Measure is, by default, aggregated, contains quantitative information, and is almost always numeric.

 You can easily see whether a field is aggregated by looking at its corresponding pill when you use it on a shelf. If it is aggregated, the name of the field is between brackets, with the name of the aggregation at the beginning (for example, SUM(Profit)).

As you can see, it's hard to give an exact rule to discern Measure and Dimension. It's more a concept to understand and a useful way to arrange the fields. Don't worry; it won't prevent you from starting to use Tableau, but understanding the difference will help you when you face your first challenges!

Yes, you could have believed that Dimensions are blue, and Measures are green. It is an easy mistake to make when you start using Tableau. Are you curious to know the real difference between the blue and green fields? Everything is explained in the next topic.

# Blue and green – Discrete and Continuous

A field or pill in blue is *Discrete*. A field or pill in green is *Continuous*. Dimensions and Measures can be either Continuous or Discrete.

A Discrete field displays each **distinct** value. Any data types can be expressed in a discrete way. In the View, a Discrete field placed in **Rows** or **Columns** is represented with headers.

Here is an example of a Dimension (**Order Date**) and a Discrete Measure (**Profit**) both as Discrete pills. As you can see, they both have clickable and distinct headers:

A Continuous field represents values from an infinite set. Only Numbers and Dates can be Continuous. In the View, Continuous fields are represented on an **axis**. Here is an example using the same Dimension (**Order Date**) and Measure (**SUM(Profit)**) fields, but this time as Continuous pills. As you can see, both are displayed using an axis:

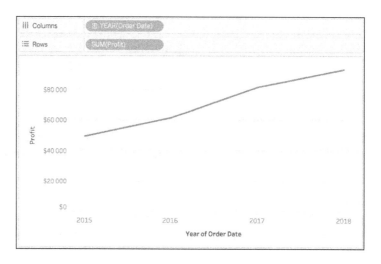

It is crucial to understand these differences. It may sound a bit abstract, but it'll help you when you start building visualizations.

Speaking of visualizations, there is a bar that you constantly see when using Tableau: the **toolbar**. Let's see some of the options available with a single click.

# The toolbar options

Whether you are working on a Worksheet, Dashboard, or Story, you can always see the toolbar on top. Let's review some of the most important and useful options it offers (and don't worry, we'll use them all in the next chapters):

- **Undo** ←: This reverses your action. The great thing is that you can undo an unlimited number of times, starting back from the very beginning if you want!

- **Add a new Data Source** ⛁ : This opens the menu to choose a new connection to a file or a server.

- **Duplicate Worksheet** : This creates a copy of the current Worksheet.

- **Clear** : This removes the pills and formatting in the Worksheet. You can use the arrow to clear only specific parts.

- **Swap** ⟳ : This replaces the pills in Rows with those in the Columns and vice versa.

- **Sort ascending/descending** ⬇ : This automatically sorts the selected Dimension.

- **Show Labels** Ⓣ : This is a shortcut to display the labels.

- **Fit** Standard ▾ : This defines how the Worksheet should fit on the screen. For **Standard**, the size of the cells defines the size of the visualization. The other fitting options force the view to fit the width, the height, or both.

- **Show Me** Show Me: This lets you change the visualization in the Worksheet at any time.

Before we finish this chapter, it's important to understand one last fundamental element of Tableau, and, more specifically, your data source: the difference between a **Live** connection and an **Extract**.

# Live or Extract

When you connect to a file or a server, on the data source workplace, in the top-right corner, you have the option to use a **Live** or **Extract** connection, as you can see in the following screenshot:

There is a big difference between these two options, so let's look at them in detail.

# Live

A Live connection creates a direct link between the Tableau data source and your data (server or file). It means that, if the data changes, you see the impact in Tableau directly after actualizing the data source, or when you reopen the workbook.

The problem with a Live connection is that you are dependent on the performance of the database. Large text files, big Excel files, or an unoptimized database can be very slow to analyze in Tableau. Also, if you are connected to an online database, you are dependent on the internet connection, and you won't be able to work offline. Every time you use a field from your data source, Tableau sends a query to the database, meaning that if there are hundreds of Tableau users, the database can rapidly be impacted. For these reasons, I advise you to always work with an Extract.

# Extract

When you create an Extract, Tableau copies your database into a `.hyper` file on your computer. Then, the data source is no longer linked to the database but to the `.hyper` file.

The first advantage of the Extract is that it's optimized for Tableau, meaning that irrespective of the speed of your initial connection, you will have excellent performance. Keep that in mind. If you think that your Dashboard is slow, the first thing to check is whether you are using an Extract or not. You are also able to work offline because the Extract is a local copy of your database.

Unlike a Live connection, you don't instantly observe the changes in the database. To see the changes, you need to refresh the Extract (recreate the `.hyper` file). When you refresh the Extract, Tableau connects to the database again and creates a new copy of the data into the `.hyper` file.

The only problem you may encounter is when you try to create an Extract from a huge database. As Tableau needs to copy the data, it could take a long time to retrieve all the rows. To deal with this, you can use the **Edit** button (next to Extract) to add filters, aggregation, and choose the schema. If you create a data source combining multiple tables, it could be better to use the **Multiple Tables** schema for better performance.

There are pros and cons of using either a Live or Extract connection. In the end, the choice is yours, but now you can make the best decision.

# Summary

This chapter is theoretical but also necessary. The rest of the book is filled with concrete examples based on real cases. However, like every tool, it is important to understand the core principle to build great visualizations. Of course, Tableau is easy, and you can start creating visualizations without any help. However, there is nothing worse than starting with bad habits, only to discover that you've been doing it wrong the whole time.

What we looked at in this chapter is the core of Tableau and how it works. We got a clear overview of the different products, learned the Tableau language and the toolbar options, and understood the difference between Measures, Dimensions, Discrete fields, Continuous fields, a Live connection, and an Extract.

How about we start using Tableau now? Isn't that why you bought this book! The next chapter is all about showing you how to build great things.

# 3
# Getting Started with Tableau Desktop

This chapter is your first concrete introduction to Tableau Desktop. Together, we'll connect to data, create three visualizations, and assemble them into what will be your first Dashboard. Then, we'll use Tableau as a data exploration tool and answer business questions by using only the power of data visualization.

In this chapter, we'll cover the following topics:

- Connecting to data
- Creating your first set of visualizations
- Building your first Dashboard
- Using Tableau Desktop for data exploration

There are a few things to remember before we start; don't be afraid; I repeat, don't be afraid. The following two buttons on the toolbar will always save you if something goes wrong:

- ← : This allows you to undo any actions, and, good news, it's unlimited. So, if you make a mistake, use it!

- : This allows you to start from the beginning. It removes everything in the Worksheet or Dashboard. You can start afresh if you feel stuck somewhere.

Are you ready? If so, then double-click on the Tableau icon and let's get started.

# Connecting to data

For this first guided tutorial, we are using the iconic Tableau dataset: Sample-Superstore. This dataset is an Excel file that contains data about supermarket sales in the United States. It can be found in your Tableau repository folder (which was created during the installation of the product). This dataset is easy to understand and use dataset. The Excel file is composed of three sheets: Orders, People, and Returns.

So, let's connect to this dataset. When you open Tableau, click on **Microsoft Excel** on the left-hand side:

- If you're a Mac user, navigate to **Documents | My Tableau Repository | Data Source | [Your Tableau Version] | en_US-US**, and then open the file named Sample Superstore.xls.

- If you're a Windows user, navigate to **My Documents | My Tableau Repository | Data Source | [Your Tableau Version] | en_US-US**, and then open the file named Sample Superstore.xls.

 If you can't find the file, then you can download it from **Chapter 3: Getting Started with Tableau,** on my website (https://tableau2019. ladataviz.com/) or by using this direct link: https://ladataviz. com/wp-content/uploads/2018/09/Sample-Superstore.xlsx. Then, select the downloaded file when connecting from Tableau.

After selecting the file, you will automatically enter the data source workplace. In the top-left of the screen, you will see the name of the connection and, underneath it, you will see the three sheets in the Excel file: **Orders**, **People**, and **Returns**.

For this example, we'll only use **Orders**; so, follow Tableau's invitation and drag the **Orders** table into the middle of the page:

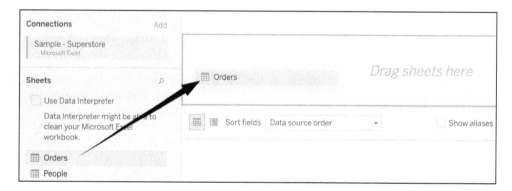

Once it's done, Tableau gives you a snapshot of the first 1,000 rows. You can also see that, preceding each column's name, there is an icon that indicates the data type (such as Number, Text, and Date) defined by Tableau.

Bravo! You've built your first data source. In the following chapters, we'll examine the meaning of each data type and the other options that are available when connecting to data in detail. For the moment, keep everything as it is and, at the bottom of the page, click on **Sheet 1**.

# Creating your first set of visualizations

After clicking on **Sheet 1**, you will enter the Worksheet workplace. This is where you create visualizations. Usually, one Worksheet answers one question.

Let's create our first visualization.

# Sales and profit by sub-categories – bar charts

The first question is: *What are the product sub-categories that generate the most sales and profits?* To answer this, perform the following steps:

1.  Double-click on **Sales** in the **Data** pane under **Measures**. You should now see one bar. If you hover the mouse over the bar, you should read **Sales: 2,297,201**. As a measure is always aggregated, here, you can see the total sum of all the sales.

2.  On the **Data** pane, under **Dimensions**, double-click on **Sub-Category**. The sub-categories now split the bar. A quick look at this can tell you that Chairs and Phones are the best-selling products:

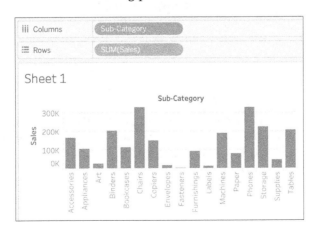

3. On the toolbar, click on the swap icon (⟳). By doing this, it's easier to read the sub-categories. We can do even better by clicking on the descending sort icon (↓⫿). The final result should be as follows:

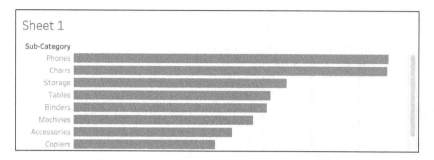

Now that the sub-categories are sorted, it's very simple to answer questions such as *What are the top three sub-categories?*, *What are the bottom three sub-categories?*, and *How do tables perform compared to bookcases?*. So, let's continue by adding in the profits.

4. In Tableau, it's straightforward to use preattentive attributes (such as **Color, Size, Shape**, and more) in order to add secondary information. Here, simply drag and drop **Profit** in the **Color** property:

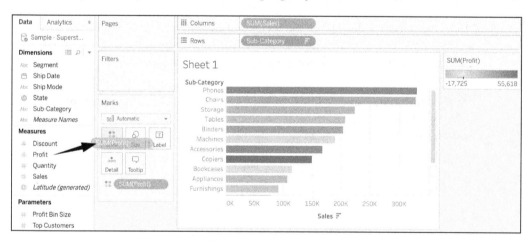

Tableau automatically uses a diverging color palette: orange for negative values and blue for positive values. So, now we can also see that **Tables, Bookcases**, and **Supplies** lose the company money.

Tableau's default color choice is adapted for colorblind people. It's a bad habit to use red and green for negative and positive values because colorblind people can't see the difference between them. If the only way to understand something is by its color, then make sure that everyone can see the difference.

Let's finish this first visualization, as follows:

5.  At the very bottom of the screen, double-click on **Sheet 1**, which is next to the **Data Source** tab, and rename the worksheet `Sales and Profit by Sub-Category`. It's crucial to give a name to each of your Worksheets in Tableau (*you'll thank me later!*).

With a few clicks and one drag and drop later, you have just created your first visualization in Tableau – congratulations! Are you ready for the next one?

# Profit evolution – line charts

Let's take a look at how the profit evolves. To build this new analysis and answer new questions, we need to create a new Worksheet. In Tableau, there is always more than one way to do something. To create a new Worksheet, you have at least three options by clicking on one of the following buttons:

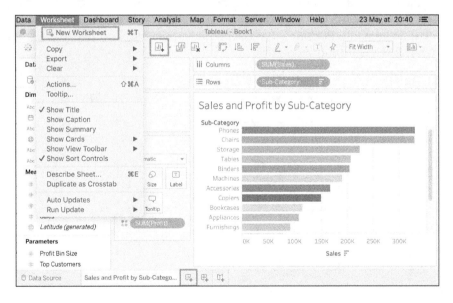

On your new Sheet 2, execute the following steps:

1. Double-click on **Profit**.

2. Double-click on **Order date**. Tableau automatically transforms the bar into a line, as follows:

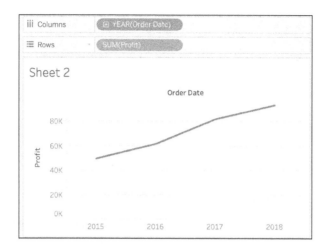

Here, you can see a line because, depending on the data type you use, Tableau selects the best way to visualize it. Of course, that can be changed, but it's too soon for that young Padawan! Here, you can see the year-by-year evolution; you will notice that the profit is growing, and that's great! But what if we want more details?

3. Right-click on the **YEAR (Order Date)** pill in the **Columns** shelf and select the second instance of **Quarter**, where you will see **Q2 2015**:

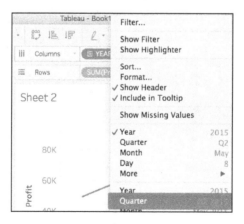

For each Date field, Tableau generates all the hierarchy: year, month, quarter, and week. The date parts in the first section are Discrete and don't include the year. For example, the Discrete Quarter only shows four values: Q1, Q2, Q3, and Q4, no matter the year. The date parts in the second section are Continuous and include the year as in this example. They are useful for you to examine evolution over time.

You can now see the quarterly evolution of the profit and discover that the fourth quarter is always the best:

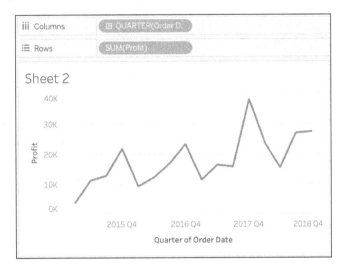

4. Rename Sheet 2 as `Profit Evolution`. Just like we did previously, double-click on the Worksheet name at the bottom of the screen.
   Note: if you change the title which appears on top of the visualization, it doesn't affect the name of the Worksheet.

So, how was that second experience? I'm sure you will love using dates in Tableau! Let's finish with my favorite topic: maps!

# Profit by state – filled maps

Are you ready for the third and final visualization of this tutorial? We are going to examine where the profit is generated and use Tableau's mapping features:

1. Start by creating a new Worksheet.

[  Hint: An easy way to do this is to click on the new Worksheet icon, which appears at the bottom of the screen ( ⊞ ). ]

2. Double-click on **State**. Tableau automatically puts **Longitude (generated)** in Columns and **Latitude (generated)** in Rows and generates a map. Each point represents a State.

3. Drag and drop **Profit** in the **Color** property. The following screenshot displays the final result:

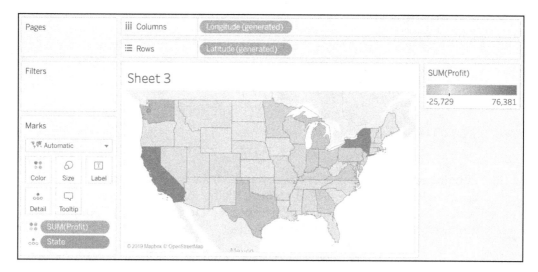

You can visually (and easily) see that the states of New York and California generate the most profit and Texas generates the highest loss of money.

4. Rename the Worksheet `Profit by State`.

Congratulations! You have just built three visualizations to analyze your supermarket sales and profit in the following way:

- By sub-categories using a bar chart
- Over time, that is, quarterly, using a line chart
- By state, using a filled map

It's now time to build your first Dashboard. By doing so, you'll be able to make your Worksheets communicate and enhance your analysis capabilities.

# Building your first Dashboard

Creating a new Dashboard is as simple as creating a new Worksheet. Choose one of the following options (and find your new favorite one!):

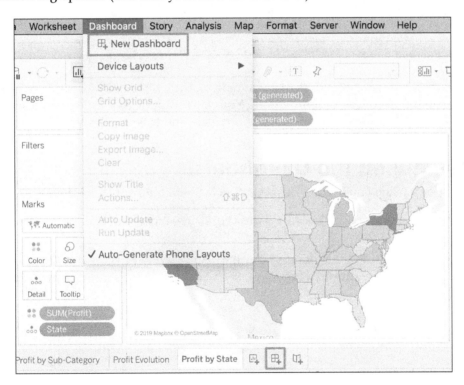

Welcome to the Dashboard workplace:

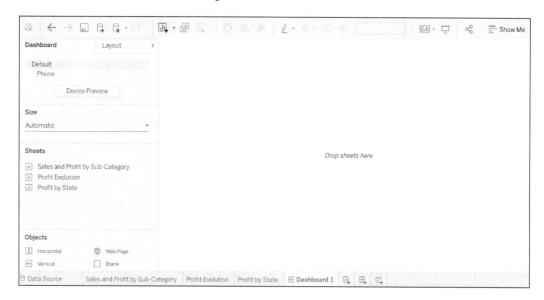

Do you see the three Worksheets that you built on the left? I hope you now understand why renaming them was very important. You don't want many Worksheets named **Sheet 1, Sheet 2, Sheet 3**, and so on. I've been there and trust me, it's a nightmare!

# Assembling the Dashboard

The first step when you build a Dashboard is to assemble your Worksheets:

1.  Drag and drop the **Profit by State** Worksheet where Tableau invites you to do so.

2.  Drag and drop the **Sales and profit by Sub-Category** Worksheet beneath the map. The gray area helps you see where the Worksheets are going to be placed:

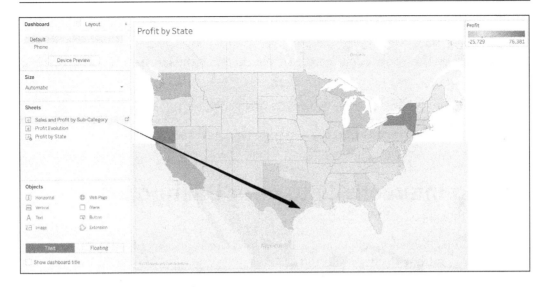

3. Drag and drop the **Profit Evolution** Worksheet on the right-hand side of **Sales and profit by Sub-Category**. Again, use the gray area to preview the location, as demonstrated in the following screenshot:

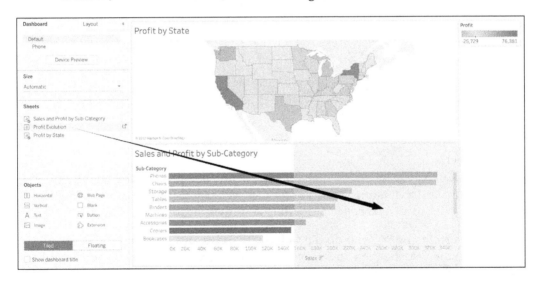

4. Double-click on **Dashboard 1** at the bottom and rename your Dashboard `Sales and profit analysis`.

5. Click on the **Show dashboard title** checkbox on the left-hand pane to display the title.

Congratulations – you've built your first Dashboard!

So, is that it? Of course not—the magic starts in the next section.

# Adding interactivity to your Dashboard

Be careful; this is going to be quick:

1. On the Dashboard, click on the **Profit by State** Worksheet to select it (there is a gray outline once it's selected).

2. Click on the funnel icon, that is, the third one that appears. Notice that it turns white once you've clicked on it. The icon is highlighted in the following screenshot:

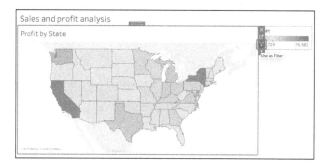

3. Click on any state on the map and be proud! You just created an interactive dashboard that automatically filters a selected state. You can also use the *Ctrl* (on Windows) or *command* (on Mac) keys to select multiple states.

Well, why stop there? You can do the same with **Sales and profit by Sub-Category**. Just click on the visualization, and then on the funnel icon, and voilà—you can filter the Dashboard by sub-category.

The Dashboard tutorial is now over. I hope that you are as amazed as I was the first time someone showed me how to build a Dashboard in Tableau. We recommend that you don't skip the final part, where we are going to use Tableau as a data exploration tool.

# Using Tableau for data exploration

Tableau can be used to answer business questions easily and visually. In this section, we'll explore our data in order to find insights. For this example, we will use the `Sample - Superstore` dataset again. If you are starting here, please refer to the preceding section, *Connecting to data* section. If you're continuing from the previous exercise, create a new Worksheet.

Let's start by building a scatterplot. This is a visualization that allows you to analyze two measures at the same time:

1.  Double-click on **Profit**, and then on **Sales**. You should see one mark that shows the sum of sales and profits:

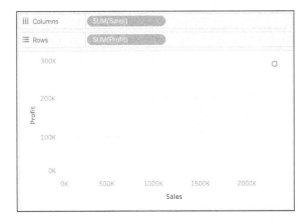

2.  Let's answer the first question: Are the unprofitable sub-categories? Drag and drop **Sub-Category** in the Label property. You should now see one mark per sub-category alongside their label (if it fits):

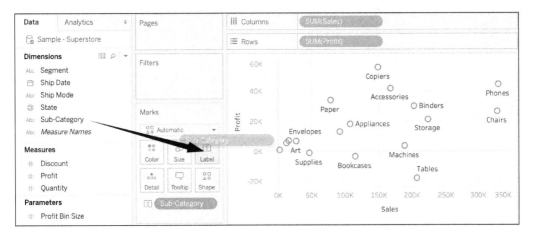

Here, **Supplies**, **Bookcases**, and **Tables** are unprofitable sub-categories. Let's go deeper into our analysis and try to understand what's happening for Tables.

3.  Click on Tables Mark and select **Keep Only**, as demonstrated in the following screenshot:

You can see that **Sub-Category** has been added to the Filters shelf. Let's continue with another question: *Are all the clients who purchased tables unprofitable?*

4.  Drag and drop **Customer Name** over **Sub-Category** to replace it, as follows:

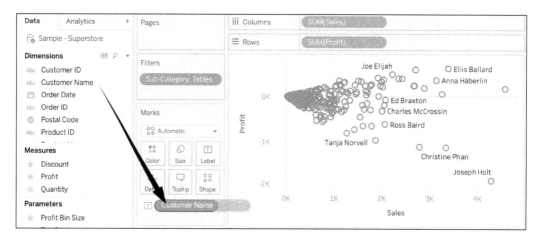

You can now see all the customers who purchased a table. A majority of clients are unprofitable, but not all.

If you want to have an even more in-depth analysis, right-click on View or on a Mark and click on **View Data...**, as displayed in the following screenshot:

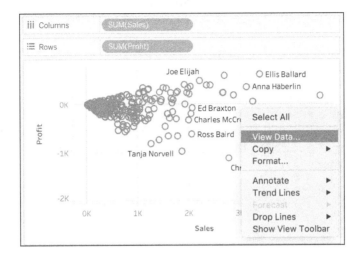

This opens a new window with, on the first tab, a **Summary** table, and on the second tab, **Full Data**, which contains all the columns and rows used by Tableau to generate the visualization:

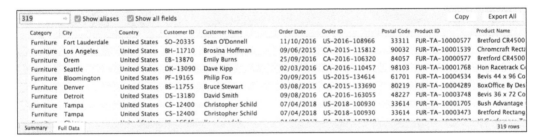

In the top-left, you have the option to export the data in CSV format if you want to share it.

As you can see, we were able to answer questions and go deeper into the analysis by staying on one Worksheet. By using the power of Tableau to visualize data, exploration is straightforward and often feels similar to a game.

Whether it was creating Dashboards or answering questions, I hope that this chapter has given you the desire to continue to discover all the great functionalities that Tableau has to offer.

# Summary

This chapter was your first concrete introduction to Tableau. I hope you enjoyed it! In this guided tutorial, you learned how to connect to an Excel file and create three Worksheets using a bar chart, a line chart, and a map. Then, you learned how to build a Dashboard and made it interactive. Finally, you explored the data to visually answer business questions.

The introduction is now over. In the following chapters, we'll focus on specific aspects of Tableau and enter the details. Speaking of what's next, I invite you to continue your journey with the next chapter. There's, you'll learn everything you need to know about connecting to any dataset, adding joins or unions, pivoting your data, and much more.

# Section 2: Connecting, Building, and Sharing

This section will give you an insight into how to connect Tableau to the dataset. We'll start by explaining the different connectors and some specificities. You will be provided with a clear description of Tableau's connections and their capabilities. The second part will demonstrate how to join data. You will understand how to create a key to connect two (or more) tables, and will also learn the differences between inner, left, right, and full joins. It's also important to explain that joining data can duplicate rows. You will receive clear explanations about the difference between live connections and extracts. After Tableau has been connected to data, we'll explore the data source in detail. It's important to understand how to design and customize a dataset. It'll help you to save a lot of time and allow you to have a comprehensive and well-built data source. We will then move on to the creation of visualizations. We'll examine different mark types, such as bar, circle, and square, and explore their usage. Then, we will focus on the options behind each property, such as the color, size, and tooltip.

Next, we will create powerful dashboards, and we will discover how to set the dashboard options. We will also demonstrate how to publish in Tableau and how to create visualizations based on published data sources.

This section will include the following chapters:

- *Chapter 4, Connecting to Data and Simple Transformations*
- *Chapter 5, Building an Efficient Data Source*
- *Chapter 6, Designing Insightful Visualizations*
- *Chapter 7, Powerful Dashboard Stories and Actions*
- *Chapter 8, Publishing and Interacting in Tableau Server*

# 4
# Connecting to Data and Simple Transformations

The first thing you usually do when opening Tableau is to connect to a dataset. You already had a glimpse of a data connection in the *previous chapter*, when we used an Excel file. In this chapter, we'll cover the most important options that Tableau offers when connecting to data, along with the following:

- Data connections
- Join data easily
- Union your data
- Simple transformations

To harmonize all the different terms used between the various data providers, we'll use the following terms through the chapter:

- **A dataset** represents any source of data. It is where your data is located. It could be an Excel file, a database on a server, or a file on the cloud. This is what you want to connect to Tableau.
- **Tables** represent, no matter the connection, a sheet in Excel or a table in a database.
- **Data Source** represents the result of your connection after all the transformations.

Let's start with some examples of data connections.

# Data connections

In this first section, we will see the general steps to follow when you want to connect to any kind of dataset. We'll also focus on connecting to spatial files.

# General rules

In this section, we'll see the general rules and options when connecting to a dataset. Of course, with more than 50 different connectors available, it's impossible to look at each in detail. However, the goals when connecting to a dataset in Tableau are always the same:

1. Choose your connection (**file/server**).
2. Connect to the dataset by selecting the file or entering the login information.
3. Reach the **Data Source** workplace and have at least one table in the area highlighted in the screenshot:

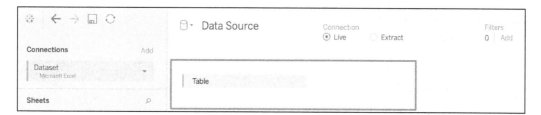

 If there is only one table in your dataset (for example, in a .CSV), Tableau automatically uses it.

Some types of connection have specificities. You can find the customization options with a right-click on the table.

For example, if you connect to a text file, say, a .CSV file, you can manually specify the field separator, the text qualifier, the character set, and the locale by using **Text File Properties...** as displayed here:

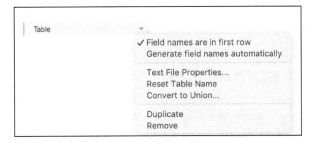

When you are connected to a server such as Redshift, SQL Server, or MySQL, you need to select the database first before getting access to the tables:

 When you connect to a server, there is a chance that the driver is not pre-installed. If so, you have to click on **Download and install the drivers** at the bottom of the connection page. You will be redirected to Tableau's website, where you can find the driver and download it.

With some servers, you can also create a custom SQL query if you have special needs. To do so, double-click on **New Custom SQL** following all the tables and write your query.

 Using a custom SQL query is slower than letting Tableau build the query with a simple drag and drop.

Tableau can connect to a lot of different data providers. They all have their specificities, but Tableau always keeps it simple.

Before starting the next section on joins, let's quickly focus on a special kind of connection: spatial files.

# Connecting spatial files

Tableau offers the possibility to connect to spatial files to display custom maps. You can use this feature to create maps with your specific territories or to add new and interesting layers of information.

When you connect to a spatial file, a special field, **Geometry**, is available in your data source. On a Worksheet, simply double-click on that field to display your custom territories. Here's an example of what you can do with spatial files, displaying the borders of the tectonic plates:

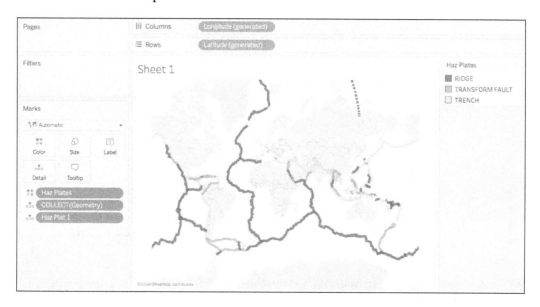

Don't hesitate to use this functionality to add roads, rivers, mountains, or special boundaries to your data.

Now that you know how to connect to different datasets, it's time to discover what you can do in the Data source workplace, starting with joins.

# Join data easily

A join creates a data source with columns coming from two (or more) tables. How can you create them? Are there risks? You'll learn everything in this section.

# The join principle

So far, we've only used one table. A join is automatically created when you drag and drop another table next to an existing one in the data source workplace. There is always a left-hand table and a right-hand table. In the following screenshot, you can see a join between **Orders** (the left-hand table), and **People** (the right-hand table):

The result of a join is a data source that contains the columns from the different joined tables. As highlighted in the screenshot, you can see that the `Profit` column comes from the `Orders` table, and the `Person` column comes from the `People` table:

There are four different types of join. We will discover these in the next section.

# Join requirements and types

To create a join between two tables, you need at least one column in each table that contains the same values. These common columns create the link between the two tables.

When you create a join, Tableau automatically uses the columns that have the same names as the links.

If there are no columns sharing the same name, you have to select the common columns manually in the **Join** menu that opens when you click on the **Join** icon. The following screenshot illustrates how you can choose the columns when you click on the icon:

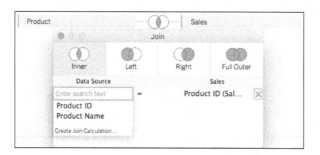

 If the values don't totally match between the common columns, you can click on **Create Join Calculation** to clean the data (you'll learn how to create a calculation in *Chapter 9, An Introduction to Calculations*).

Often, you'll have one column in each table, with only some shared values. It's up to you to decide how to deal with the values that don't match by choosing the correct join type: **Inner**, **Left**, **Right**, or **Full Outer**. To select a join type, click on one of the four icons in the **Join** menu. Here are the differences between the different type of joins:

- **Inner Join** (default): Keeps only the lines where the values match in both tables.

- **Left Join**: Keeps all the lines from the left-hand table and adds the information from the right table if the values match. If the values don't match, Tableau puts `null` in the columns coming from the right-hand table.

- **Right Join**: Keeps all the lines from the right-hand table and adds the information from the left-hand table if the values match. If the values don't match, Tableau puts `null` in the columns coming from the left-hand table.

- **Full Outer**: Keeps all the lines from the two tables. If the values don't match, Tableau enters `null`.

Enough of the theory–let's create a simple and useful join together.

# Hands-on with a simple join

In this section we'll create a join between the Orders and People tables from Sample - Superstore. Before we start, let's look at what those tables contain:

- Orders is the main table (the left-hand one). We already used it in *Chapter 3, Getting Started with Tableau Desktop*, and this contains the profit.

- People is a table that contains only four lines and two columns. It associates a region with a person.

Our goal is to create a data source that allows us to look at the profit (which exists only in the Orders table) by person (which exists only in the People table).

Open a new Tableau file and follow these instructions:

1. Select **Microsoft Excel** in the list of available connections and connect to the Sample-Superstore Excel file in your Tableau repository (use the *Connecting to data* section from *Chapter 3, Getting Started with Tableau Desktop,* if you don't remember the file's location).

2. In the **Data Source** workspace, drag and drop the Orders table.

3. Drag and drop the People table next to Orders, as shown in the following screenshot:

Tableau automatically creates a join between the two tables, with **Region** as the link, as shown in the following screenshot:

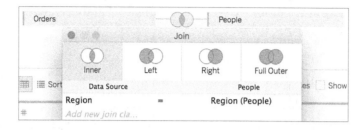

On the preview, you can see that the two new columns from the `Person` table on the right:

| # | # | Abc | Abc |
| Orders | Orders | People | People |
| **Discount** | **Profit** | **Person** | **Region (People)** |
| 0.000000 | 41.91 | Cassandra Brandow | South |
| 0.000000 | 219.58 | Cassandra Brandow | South |
| 0.000000 | 6.87 | Anna Andreadi | West |

The data source is ready. You can test it on a worksheet and display the profit by person as we wanted.

As you can see, joins are very powerful. Be careful; there are some risks.

# Join risks

The main risk with **joins** is data duplication. Rather than a theoretical explanation, consider the following example:

 If you want to reproduce the example, you can download the `Data duplication example` file from my website, `https://tableau2019.ladataviz.com`, as discussed in **Chapter 4: Connecting to Data and Simple Transformation** section, or go direct to `https://ladataviz.com/wp-content/uploads/2018/09/Data-duplication-example.xlsx`.

The `Data duplication example` Excel file contains two sheets: `Sales` and `Product`. `Sales` contains the following data:

| Product ID | Sales |
|---|---|
| 1 | 100 |
| 2 | 100 |
| 3 | 100 |

The total volume of sales is `300`.

**Product** contains the following data:

| Product ID | Product Name |
|---|---|
| 1 | Shield |
| 2 | Bow |
| 3 | Fire arrow |
| 3 | Ice arrow |

Now, let's join the two tables on the `Product ID` columns and see what happens. Here's the result in Tableau:

| Product<br>**Product ID** | Sales<br>**Product ID (Sales)** | Product<br>**Product Name** | Sales<br>**Sales** |
|---|---|---|---|
| 1 | 1 | Shield | 100 |
| 2 | 2 | Bow | 100 |
| 3 | 3 | Fire arrow | 100 |
| 3 | 3 | Ice arrow | 100 |

As you can see, the product number `3` is duplicated. The reason for that duplication is because there are two different products in the `Product` table, with the same `Product ID`. The total volume of sales here is `400`, which is wrong.

When you join tables, be sure that the values you want to analyze won't be duplicated. There are three solutions to dealing with data duplication:

- **The easiest solution**: Clean the file to remove the duplication. In the example, it means changing the ID of a product to `4`.
- Use data blending — this is explained in *Chapter 11, Advanced Data Connections*.
- Use **Level of Detail (LOD)** calculation functions — this is explained in *Chapter 9, An Introduction to Calculations*.

After joins, the next interesting feature is **unions**.

# Union your data

If a join adds columns, a union adds rows.

Unions are useful when you have two (or more) tables with an identical structure (the same columns) that you want to combine to create a unique data source.

A typical use case is when you have a dataset that contains one table per year, and you need to compare those years. To do that, you need to combine those different tables into a single data source. You can, of course, spend some time copying and pasting the data into a new table, but with Tableau and unions, you can do this in a few clicks.

> To create a union, the different tables must contain the same column names. Otherwise, Tableau will not consider them to be identical and will create new columns.

Let's start with an example.

# Hands-on with a union example

For this example, I created an Excel file with two sheets to union.

> If you want to reproduce the example, you can download the Union example file from my website, https://tableau2019.ladataviz.com, in **Chapter 4: Connect to Data and Simple Transformation** section, or use this direct link: https://ladataviz.com/wp-content/uploads/2018/09/Union-example.xlsx.

The Union example Excel file contains two sheets:

- One named 2017, which contains the data shown in the following screenshot:

| Value | Country |
|---|---|
| 310 | United States |
| 120 | France |
| 100 | Spain |

- One named 2018, with the data shown in the following screenshot:

| Value | Country |
|---|---|
| 130 | United States |
| 60 | France |
| 940 | Spain |

As you can see, the two sheets share the same column name. In Tableau, after connecting to the Excel file, there are two ways of making a union:

- **The first way**: Drag and drop the 2017 table, then drag and drop the second table, 2018, just beneath the first one, where it says **Drag table to union**:

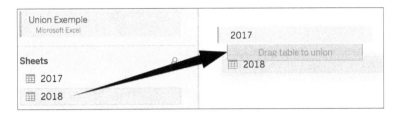

- **The second way**: Drag and drop **New Union**, as shown in the following screenshot:

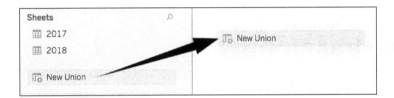

This opens a new window where you can drag and drop the two tables to union them:

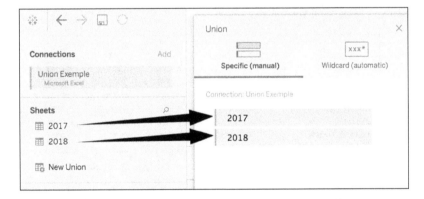

 You'll learn in *Chapter 11, Advanced Data Connection,* how to use the second tab to create wildcard unions.

No matter the way you choose to do it, the result of the union is a data source that combines the two tables. Tableau automatically creates new columns with the name of the origin table. The following screenshot displays the final result of the union:

| Union Value | Union Country | Union Sheet | Union Table Name |
|---|---|---|---|
| 310 | United States | 2017 | 2017 |
| 120 | France | 2017 | 2017 |
| 100 | Spain | 2017 | 2017 |
| 130 | United States | 2018 | 2018 |
| 60 | France | 2018 | 2018 |
| 940 | Spain | 2018 | 2018 |

To end this chapter about data connections, let's look at some of the transformations that you can apply to the data source.

# Simple transformations

Tableau is not a data preparation tool. It's always better to have a clean file to start with. However, Tableau offers some simple transformation tools. When you connect to a dataset, you can, for example, use the **Data Interpreter**, split a column into multiple columns, or pivot your data. Let's see a case for these transformations.

For this section, I created a dataset to clean in Excel, as illustrated here:

| Country and City | Year 2015 | 2016 | 2017 | 2018 |
|---|---|---|---|---|
| Kenya/Nairobi | 74271 | 13190 | 40746 | 22826 |
| Brazil/Rio | 52579 | 17388 | 30067 | 1849 |
| United States/Denver | 21691 | 7765 | 44720 | 3394 |
| Germany/Berlin | 47946 | 43622 | 19961 | 2537 |
| Japan/Tokyo | 5072 | 49598 | 29861 | 33979 |
| Finland/Helsinki | 59153 | 80023 | 61742 | 65594 |
| Russia/Moscow | 22697 | 38769 | 21267 | 12695 |
| Norway/Oslo | 61135 | 20984 | 42127 | 28246 |

If you want to reproduce the example, you can download the `Dataset to clean` file from my website, `https://tableau2019.ladataviz.com`, as discussed in **Chapter 4: Connecting to Data and Simple Transformation** section, or use this direct link: `https://ladataviz.com/wp-content/uploads/2018/09/Data-duplication-example.xlsx`.

Three things are problematic with this dataset:

- There is a column header for the years
- The countries and the cities are in the same column
- Each year is in a different column, preventing the creation of a simple line chart

Now, let's fix the first problem of this dataset with the Data Interpreter.

# The Data Interpreter

Let's start by connecting to the Dataset to clean file in Tableau:

1. Open Tableau, select **Microsoft Excel** in the list of connectors, and select the Dataset to clean Excel file.

2. Tableau automatically puts the unique sheet, **Sales**, in the **Data** pane, but, as you can see in the preview, the connection needs cleansing:

3. To clean the file, click on **Use Data Interpreter** underneath **Sheets**. As you can see in the following screenshot, it's already much better:

However, we still need to split the Country and City column and pivot the years.

# Splitting a column

The second goal is to split the Country and City column into two columns:

1.  Right-click on the Country and City column and click on **Split.**

2.  Tableau automatically recognizes that there is a common character and uses it to split the column into two new ones, Country and City-Split 1, and Country and City-Split 2.

3.  Right-click on the new columns and select **Rename**. Rename the first one Country, and the second one City.

The result is displayed in the following table:

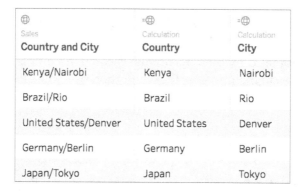

| ⊕ Sales Country and City | =⊕ Calculation Country | =⊕ Calculation City |
|---|---|---|
| Kenya/Nairobi | Kenya | Nairobi |
| Brazil/Rio | Brazil | Rio |
| United States/Denver | United States | Denver |
| Germany/Berlin | Germany | Berlin |
| Japan/Tokyo | Japan | Tokyo |

 If Tableau cannot find a character for the split, or if Tableau chooses the wrong one, you can use a custom split to have advanced options. Selecting **Custom Split...** opens a window where you can choose the separator and the number of columns.

That's two problems fixed! Let's finish with the pivot.

# Pivot

A pivot consists of transforming columns into lines. In this example, we want to pivot the four columns with the different years into two columns: one for the name of the year and one for the value.

To do this, follow these steps:

1.  Select all the year columns to pivot (click on them while pressing
    *Ctrl* (Windows) or *command* (macOS)).

2.  Right-click on one of the highlighted columns and select **Pivot**,
    as highlighted here:

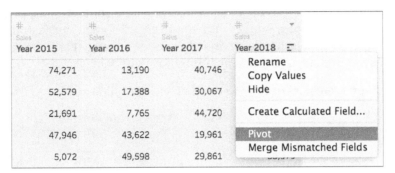

The result of the pivot is two columns:

-   **One Dimension**: `Pivot Field Names`
-   **One Measure**: `Pivot Field Values`

You can rename them `Year` and `Value` respectively.

The transformations are complete. You have a clean and simple data source.
To really make it perfect, you can click on the icon of the `Year` column and change
it to `Date`. Here's the final result:

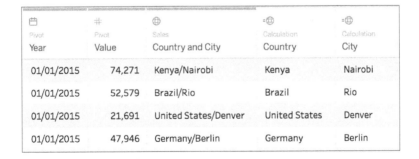

As you can see, you can even use Tableau to clean your data very quickly!

# Summary

We have finished our first chapter about data connections. We looked at how to connect to different sorts of datasets and use some features, such as join, union, and some data transformations. Later in the book, you'll learn other useful and powerful data transformation features.

Now that you are connected to the data, you have a data source. You can directly use it to create visualizations, but I advise you to spend some time customizing and preparing your data source. There are many ways to enhance it and create something shareable, easy to understand, and compelling for your analysis.

In the next chapter, we'll learn how to build an efficient data source.

# 5
# Building an Efficient Data Source

The data source is a crucial part of Tableau. In fact, the data source is the engine of Tableau that allows you to build visualizations. It affects the performance, the quality of the analysis, the speed, and more. Additionally, like any engine, it's necessary to spend some time taking care of it.

In this chapter, you'll learn how to build the best possible engine for your analysis. We will cover the following topics:

- Understanding the data source
- Refreshing a data source and dealing with changes
- Field customization and default properties
- Hierarchies
- Groups, sets, and bins

Let's start with a clear explanation of what a data source is.

## Understanding the data source

The data source is the result of all your work when connecting to a dataset (such as joins, unions, and transformations), and all the customizations that you can apply afterward. The goal for your data source is to be as performant, simple, and easy-to-use as possible.

A data source can be a Live connection (⬦), an Extract (⬦), or it can be published on Tableau Server (⬦). However, no matter what type of connection it is, you will always find the same elements.

There are four elements that make up a data source: **Dimensions**, **Measures**, **Sets**, and **Parameters**. Dimensions and Measures are always present and are linked to the field in your dataset.

 It's essential to understand the difference between Dimensions and Measures. Everything about these two elements is explained in *Chapter 2, The Tableau Core*.

Sets and Parameters are optional, and they are created by you. Sets are explained in the *Groups, sets, and bins* section, and there is a focus on parameters in *Chapter 10, Analytics and Parameters*.

Let's continue with an overview of the different data types.

# Data types in Tableau

Each field has a data type. There are seven data types in Tableau, as follows:

- Text ( Abc ), which is also called a **string**
- Number, decimal, or whole ( # ) — these data types all share the same icon.
- Date ( 📅 )
- Date and time ( 📅 )
- Boolean ( T|F ) — this value will either be true or false
- Geographic values ( 🌐 )

When you connect to a dataset, Tableau automatically chooses a type for each column of the dataset. However, as with almost everything in Tableau, you can customize it. To change the data type, you can either click on the icon, or right-click on the field and use **Change Data Type**.

Most of the fields in your data source come from the dataset. However, did you notice that some of these don't? Continue reading to learn more about generated information.

# Generated information

Every data source can have up to five generated pieces of information:

- **Number of records**: You can use this to find out how many lines are analyzed.

- **Latitude (generated) and Longitude (generated)**: You'll find this information if you have a geographical field in your data source. They are used to create maps.

- **Measure Names and Measure Values**: The first one contains the name of each measure, and the second one contains the values of each measure. They must be combined and you can use them to display multiple Measures at the same time (this is a focus of *Chapter 6, Design Insightful Visualizations*).

Now that you have a clear view of what exists in your data source, let's take a look at the options to customize it.

# Data source options

All the data source options are available by right-clicking on the name in the top-left corner of the screen:

You can also access them by clicking on **Data** in the top-left menu.

Here's a brief description of the most important options:

- **Edit Data Source...**: This takes you to the data source page, where you can change your connection, add new tables, or do some transformations.

- **Refresh**: This refreshes your data if you are using a Live connection.

- **View Data**: This opens a window where you can view your raw data, copy it, or export it in a CSV file.

- **Close**: This removes your data source. It also removes all the Worksheets with a visualization based on that data source.

- **Extract Data**: This opens a new window where you can configure the extract and create it.

- **Extract...**: This submenu is available when you are using an Extract and allows you to refresh it, append data from a file, or show the history.

- **Edit Data Source Filters**: This opens a new window where you can add some filters (more details on this can be found in *Chapter 6, Design Insightful Visualizations.*

> You can also add a data source filter in the **Data Source** page, in the top-right, next to the menu where you select **Live** or **Extract**.

- **Replace Data Source**: This opens a menu where you can select the current and the replacement data source. All the Worksheets that use the current source will use the replacement one.

- **Date Properties**: This allows you to change three options, including the week's starting day, the fiscal year start, and the default date format.

- **Edit Aliases**: This allows you to add an alias to the values of a dimension.

- **Add to Saved Data Source**: This allows you to export the data source as a file for further usage.

- **Export Data to CSV**: This exports the data in a CSV file. However, be careful when using this option; if you have a large data source, then the export can be very long.

You don't have to remember all of these options. Bear in mind that if you want to do something related to your data source, it's probably one right-click away.

In the next section, we'll explore in detail how to refresh your data and deal with the changes.

# Refreshing a data source and dealing with changes

Data lives and changes. Any analysis tool, such as Tableau, needs to allow users to refresh data and deal with changes as easily as possible.

In this section, we won't talk about the published data source on Tableau Server. The way in which to refresh or modify a published data source is different and is explained in more detail in *Chapter 8, Publishing and Interacting in Tableau Server*.

The following section describes how to refresh a data source.

# How to refresh a data source

Refreshing a data source is simple for both Live and Extract data sources.

For a Live connection, right-click on the data source and click on **Refresh**—that's it!

For an Extract, clicking on **Refresh** won't work because the extracted data (in the hyper file) hasn't changed. Remember that when you create an Extract, you create a copy of your dataset. To refresh an Extract data source, you first need to refresh the extracted data. To do so, right-click on the data source name, go to **Extract**, and then **Refresh**, as demonstrated in the following screenshot:

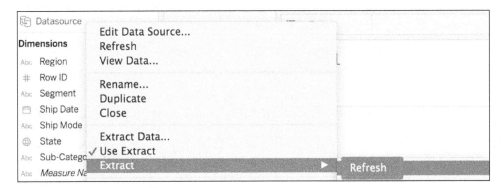

When refreshing an extract, Tableau warns you that the data will change. If you click on **Yes** to continue, Tableau connects to the dataset and imports the data again. At the end of the extraction, your extract is refreshed.

But what happens if there are some modifications in the dataset between the two refreshes?

# Dealing with changes

Again, Tableau is here to help you if there are changes made to the dataset. Note that not all changes will cause a problem.

Here are two trivial cases for you to consider:

- **A new column is added to the dataset**: If there is a new column in the dataset, then you'll see a new field in the data source. In this case, you don't have to do anything.

- **An unused field is removed or renamed**: If there is an unused field in your data source that is deleted or renamed from the dataset, you won't even notice it. It'll simply be suppressed or renamed.

- The third and last case, when a field that you use in Tableau is deleted or renamed in the dataset, is a bit more problematic.

If a field that you use in Tableau is removed or renamed in the dataset, there will be an exclamation point next to its name after refreshing the Data pane. If the column is removed, you can't do anything except put it back. Most of the time, the column is just renamed, and, in Tableau, you can replace the references to the old column with the new one.

Let me illustrate the process using the Sample - Superstore dataset. Let's say that the Region column was renamed New Region:

1. When I refresh the data source, the **Region** pill turns red, and in the **Datasource** pane, there is an exclamation mark next to the **Region** field:

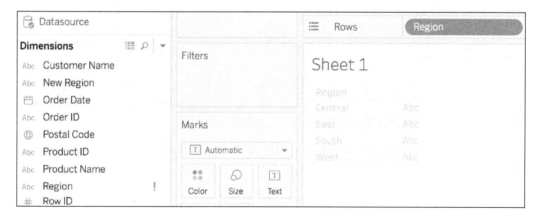

2.  In order to correct the error, I can right-click on the **Region** field and select **Replace References...**:

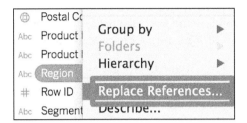

3.  Then, I select the new field that replaces the old one. In this example, it's New Region.

4.  The old field, Region, is removed from the data source and, in the Worksheets, the pill is now using New Region. You can see the result in the following screenshot:

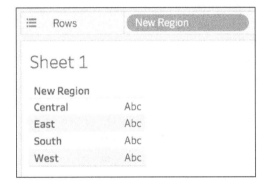

Easy, isn't it? Now that you have a clear view of how to use and refresh your data source, it's time to explore how you can customize it.

# Field customization and default properties

Customizing the data source is the best way to make it easier to use and share. Let's take a look at the different options available to transform a raw data source into a customized one.

First, let's do a tour of the different field options, and then focus on the default properties.

## Field customization options

All the field customization options are available with a right-click on any field.

There are some straightforward options, so let's take a look at a short description of those that aren't trivial:

- **Hide**: This hides the field but doesn't suppress it. It's a great way to clean your data source if there are many fields that you won't use. The option is only available if the field is never used. You can show the hidden field by clicking on the arrow next to **Dimension** and selecting **Show Hidden Fields**.

- **Delete**: This suppresses custom fields (such as Bins, Sets, or Parameters) from the data source.

- **Aliases...**: This allows you to rename the values of a Dimension. It opens a new window with the list of the values and a column to specify the alias.

- **Create**: This opens a submenu where you can create new fields. All the different options will be examined in detail in this book.

- **Convert to Discrete or Convert to Continuous**: This only applies to numbers and allows you to switch from a Continuous field to a Discrete field or vice versa.

- **Convert to Dimension or Convert to Measure**: This allows you to switch from a Measure to a Dimension or vice versa. If you try to convert anything other than a number from a Dimension to a Measure, then an aggregation is automatically applied.

- **Geographical Role**: The geographical role is available on a text dimension and allows you to specify a geographical role if Tableau doesn't recognize it automatically.

- **Group by**: This opens a submenu where you can select **Folder** or **Data Source Table**. It affects the way Tableau organizes the dimension and measure. With **Data Source Table**, the fields are linked to their tables. With **Folder**, all the fields are mixed, and you can create folders to group them using the next **Folders...** option.

Again, you don't have to remember everything. Bear in mind that if you want to change or customize something related to a field, then you'll surely find it with a simple right-click on the field.

Some of these options require more explanation. So, let's start with default properties.

# Default properties

With this option, you can define the default properties for your fields. The properties are a slightly different between Measures and Dimensions:

- **Comment...** adds a comment to a field that appears when you hover over it with your mouse; consider the following example:

  This option is relatively useful if anyone other than you is going to use the data source. This is because they'll be able to see the comment and have a better understanding of the field.

- **Color...** is really important in data visualizations. With this default property, you can predefine the color for each value if the field is a dimension, or the default palette if the field is a measure. This option is a time saver; when you use a field with a default color, you won't have to assign them again.

- The **Shape...** default property works in the same way as the **Color** property. The only difference is that you are not affecting different colors, but different shapes instead. Every time you use a field with a **Shape** default property in **Shape**, Tableau uses the ones that you have assigned.

- The **Sort...** default property opens a new window where you can specify the sort order. You can choose between three options: **Data source order**, **Alphabetic**, or **Manual sort**. After defining the default sort option, Tableau will always display the values in the order that you specified.

- The **Number format...** property allows you to specify the format of numbers. When you click on the option, this is the menu that opens:

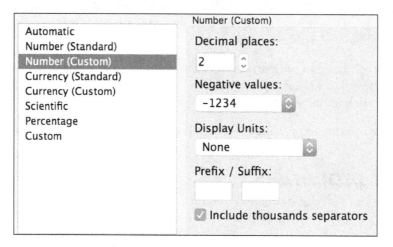

- You can use the menu to choose between the four main formats: **Number**, **Currency**, **Scientific**, and **Percentage**. Alternatively, you can add a **Custom** format. When you select **Number (Custom)** or **Currency (Custom)**, you have a few options to create the format of your choice. Once you specify a default format, Tableau will use it every time you use the measure.

- As you know, Tableau aggregates the measure when you use it. By default, Tableau usually uses a sum. With the **Aggregation** default property, you can change this. For example, you can change the default aggregation of a measure to be the average. **Total using** is quite similar: here, you can specify the aggregation used to display totals.

That's it for the default properties. These options are used to increase your speed in Tableau and are useful if you want to share your data source. Another great way to customize your data source is to add hierarchies.

# Hierarchies

Hierarchies are quite special. A hierarchy is a group of multiple dimensions. However, a hierarchy doesn't just affect the data source, but also the visualization and the way the users can interact with it. A hierarchy creates a relationship between different dimensions, such as a parent-child relationship.

The dedicated icon for **Hierarchies** is  .

>
> Hierarchies are crucial for geographical roles. If you try to
> build a visualization in a city level without a hierarchy, lots of
> cities won't be displayed because their names are ambiguous
> (that is, they exist in multiple countries). By creating a
> hierarchy with a country-level field and a region-level field,
> there is no more ambiguity.

Dates, for example, are a hierarchy. A day is included in a week, which is included
in a month and a year. If you use a date in a Worksheet, then Tableau automatically
selects the **YEAR** and shows a small **+** in the pill, on the left-side of its name. This
means that the dimension is a parent in a hierarchy where there are children. This is
illustrated in the following screenshot:

Once you click on the **+** icon, the child dimension is added next to the parent, and
the **+** icon switches to a **-** icon. The child can also be a parent of another dimension,
and so on.

That's enough for the theory; let's create a hierarchy and use it. You can reproduce
the following example using the `Sample - Superstore` dataset:

1. Select **Category** and **Sub-Category**.

2. Right-click on one of the selected Dimensions and go to **Hierarchy**, and
   then click on **Create Hierarchy...**.

3. A new window opens asking for the name of the hierarchy; let's name
   it `Products`.

4. The hierarchy is created, and you should see a new icon in your **Data** pane,
   with the **Category** and **Sub-Category** fields under it. Your hierarchy should
   look similar to the following screenshot:

>
> If the order is different, then you can easily drag and drop the
> field to change the order.

5.  Let's add **Product Name** in the hierarchy, at the bottom. To do that, you can drag and drop the field under **Sub-Category**:

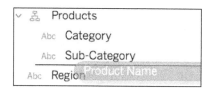

6.  Double-click on **Category**, and then on **Profit**. This creates a simple table. You can see the **+** icon next to the **Category** pill. You can also see the **+** icon when you hover over the values in View:

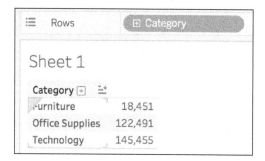

7.  Click on **+**; Tableau automatically adds the child, **Sub-Category**. From here, you can go deeper in the **Product Name** field using **+,** or remove **Sub-Category** using **-**.

Hierarchies are useful and powerful tools. We recommend that you use them when you can. Let's finish this chapter with the final option: creating groups, sets, and bins.

# Groups, sets, and bins

Groups, sets, and bins are synonyms, but they are fundamentally different in Tableau:

-   Groups and sets are created from D**imensions**. In comparison to this, bins are created from measures.

-   Groups and bins are **Dimensions**, but sets are a different Tableau element (such as Dimensions and Measures).

Are you a bit lost? Don't worry, that's normal! Let's take a look at some examples that you can reproduce using the Sample-Superstore dataset. We'll start with groups.

# Groups

A group is a way to create a new dimension that gathers different values of another dimension. Additionally, a group is static; this means that you need to modify it manually.

A group is characterized by the ⫞ icon.

There are two ways to create a group; first, **manually**, with a menu—this is for when you know in advance how to gather the values. Second, you can create a group **visually** in the View.

Let's start by creating a group, manually, with `Sample - Superstore`:

1. Right-click on **Sub-Category**, go to **Create**, and then click on **Group**. A new window opens where you see the list of the values in that Dimension. In this menu, you can manage the groups.

2. To create a new group of values, select some values and click on the **Group** button at the bottom (or with a right-click). Then, create a group with `Tables` and `Chairs`, as demonstrated in the following screenshot:

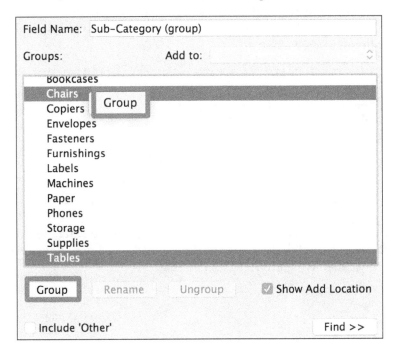

3. By default, Tableau names the group with a concatenation of the name of the values. However, it's possible to rename it by clicking on the **Rename** button. Rename the group `Desk Furniture`.

4. After clicking on **OK**, a new Dimension is created. If you didn't change the name, then it is called **Sub-Category (group)**.

5. To test the group, try creating a simple visualization—double-click on **Profit**, and then double-click on **Sub-Category (group)**. You should see your new group, `Desk Furnitures`, among the list.

If you have too many values and you want to group them, you can use the visual way. Let's demonstrate how to do this with `Sample - Superstore`:

1. On a new Worksheet, double-click on **Sales**, and then double-click on **Sub-Category** to create a simple visualization.

2. Use the button in the toolbar to swap (  ) and sort (  ) the values as descending. As you can see, there are some sub-categories with small sales. They are not important, so we will want to group them together.

3. Select the five bottom values by clicking on their names in the header (note that it is crucial that you do not select the bars). Then, in the menu that appears, click on the group icon to create a group. The icon is highlighted in the following screenshot:

4. Again, you can rename the group by editing it on the **Data** pane, or by right-clicking on it in the View to edit the aliases. Choose your favorite way and rename the group `Small Sales`.

Creating a group visually is an excellent way to reduce the number of insignificant values and to help you to focus on what matters. Another perfect use case is when there is a typo, and you want to combine the wrong value with the correct one.

As we said at the beginning, a group is not dynamic. However, sets are dynamic, so let's demonstrate how to use them.

# Sets

Sets are a Tableau element. A set is created from a Dimension. Unlike groups, sets are dynamic. With sets, the values are either **In** the set or **Out**.

Sets have a special icon: 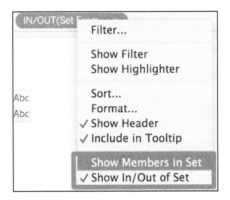.

Sets have two ways of being displayed in a Worksheet. By default, a set will return `In` or `Out`, but if you right-click on its pill, then you can see that it's possible to show the members that are in the set:

To create a set, right-click on a Dimension, go to **Create**, and then click on **Set**. A new window opens with three tabs:

- The first tab, **General**, allows you to select the values that will be in the set.

- The second tab, **Condition**, automatically puts the values in the set if the condition is fulfilled. For example, in the following screenshot, the values of the Dimension will be in the set if the **Profit** field is greater than zero:

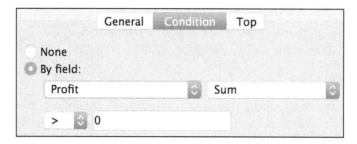

- The third tab, **Top**, puts the values in the set if they are the top (or bottom) ones based on the limit number and a Measure. This final option is used in the following example.

So, let's create a concrete sets example using `Sample - Superstore`:

1. On the **Data** pane, right-click on **State**, navigate to **Create**, and then click on **Set**.

2. A new window opens; change the name of the set to `Top 5 State by Profit`.

3. Click on the **Top** tab and select **By field**. Keep **Top** listed and write 5 instead of **10**. Then, select the **Profit** field and keep the **Sum** field for aggregation. The configuration window of your set should look like the following screenshot:

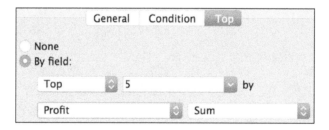

4. Click on **OK**. You should see a new set element in your data source:

5. In a new Worksheet, double-click on **State** to show a map, and then drag and drop **Top 5 State by Profit** (that is, your new set) onto **Color**, as demonstrated in the following screenshot:

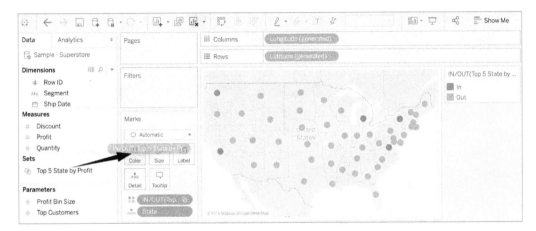

6. You should see a map with five states highlighted. These five states are the five most profitable ones.

A great feature of sets is that they are dynamic. This means that, if at the next refresh, Texas become one of the five most profitable states, its dot will automatically be highlighted.

Sets and groups are both based on Dimensions, but their use is very different to our last item — bins.

# Bins

A bin is a Dimension. Unlike groups and sets, bins are based on a Measure. The purpose of a bin is to group the different range of values of a Measure inside a bin.

Bins have a special icon: .ılı. .

As always, the best way to understand anything is with examples. So, let's create bins using `Sample - Superstore`:

1. Right-click on **Discount**, navigate to **Create**, and then click on **Bins...**.

2. A new window opens in which you can edit the bin; keep the name **Discount (bin)**. The size of the bin is automatically suggested by Tableau, but in our case, we will change the size to 0.1.

3. Click on **OK**; you will see that a new Dimension is created. You should find the **Discount (bin)** field in your data source.

4. Let's use it; double-click on **Number of Records**, and then on **Discount (bin)**. You can now easily see that the majority of the orders have less than a 10% discount, or between 20% and 30%. Here's the final result:

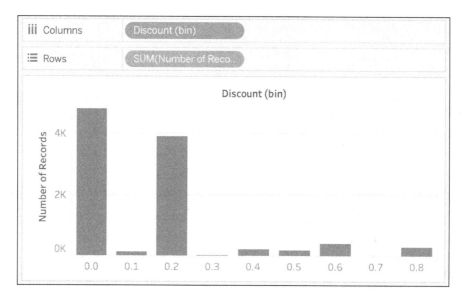

With groups, sets, and bins, we've explored three of the five field creation capabilities. The final two—Calculated Fields and Parameters—are even more powerful. But that's for *Chapter 9, An Introduction to Calculations and Chapter 10, Analytics and Parameters.*

# Summary

So, you've made it! The data source has no more surprises for you (or maybe one or two that we'll see later!).

In this chapter, you learned about the purpose of a data source, its options, how to refresh it, and how to deal with changes. Then, you learned how to customize a data source using the default properties. Finally, you created hierarchies, groups, sets, and bins.

Building the data source is not the most exciting thing to do if, like me, you love visualization. However, spending some time creating a good data source and understanding its potential is crucial if you want to create the best analysis.

Speaking of visualization, how about we start using Tableau for its primary purpose? The next chapter is all about data visualization.

# 6
# Design Insightful Visualizations

Finally! Visualization! I know it was tempting to skip the last few chapters and start here, but everything you learned earlier is crucial. That's not because you won't be able to understand this chapter, but because you'll miss an essential part of what Tableau can do for you.

Creating visualizations is the core of Tableau and there is a lot to say! In this chapter, we'll cover the following topics:

- Creating visualization
- Mark types
- Mark properties
- Using multiple measures
- Filters
- Pages
- Options and formats

In this chapter, we'll primarily use Tableau's `Sample - Superstore` saved data source for our examples. You can find it on the first page when you open Tableau, in the bottom-left of the screen:

All you need to do is to simply click on it, and then you're ready. The data source is based on the `Sample -Superstore` Excel file and uses many of the features that we saw in *Chapter 5, Building an Efficient Data Source*.

So, are you ready? Let's start with the basics, that is, how to build a visualization in Tableau.

# Creating visualizations

In Tableau, the only way to display a visualization is by adding fields in shelves. The different shelves are **Rows**, **Columns**, **Marks**, **Filters**, and **Pages**. When you use a field on a shelf, it becomes a pill.

However, there are two very different ways of adding a field to a shelf: the automatic and the manual way. The automatic way is useful when you want to go fast or if you have no idea how to visualize your data. The manual way is needed when you know exactly what you want to build.

Let's start with the automatic way.

# Building a visualization, the automatic way

There are two ways of allowing Tableau to do the job for you.

The first method is one that you've used the most frequently in this book, that is, double-click. A simple double-click on a field automatically puts it in a shelf.

## Double-click

When you double-click on a field in your data source, it is automatically added to a shelf in the Worksheet. Tableau decides where the field should be, based on data visualization best practices.

Of course, there are limitations to what you can do with double-clicks. For instance, you won't be able to create a lot of different visualizations, and you also won't be able to go outside predefined scripts—very soon, you'll feel limited.

However, a double-click is always the most efficient way to build a map. With a simple double-click on any geographical Dimension, Tableau automatically puts the latitude values in the Rows and the longitude values in the Columns.

The second method of allowing Tableau to do the work is by using **Show Me**; this is the menu that appears in the top-right side of the toolbar.

# Show Me

Show Me is a special menu that can be accessed on the top-right side of the toolbar. You can easily spot it by its icon:  Show Me . When you click on this icon, you can open or close a list of twenty-four predefined visualizations.

If no fields are selected in your data source, then all the options are grayed out. If you choose one or multiple fields, then you'll see that some options are now available. One of them will have an orange outline—this is the one that Tableau recommends that you select. To use an option, simply click on it.

Let's take a look at a quick example using `Sample - Superstore`:

1. Simultaneously select **Order Date**, **Category**, and **Profit** in the **Data** pane (using *Ctrl* or *command*).

2. Open the **Show Me** menu.

3. Click on some of the options to see different results.

Show Me is useful for when you first start in Tableau, and when you have no idea how to visualize your data. You can click on the various options to see different results and select the one that you prefer. After some time, you'll use Show Me very rarely. That's because, even if you have many possibilities, you are limited by how Tableau arranges the pill.

> Show Me is quite a powerful option to create box-and-whisker and bullet graphs. Without Show Me, these two visualizations will require lots of steps if you were to create them manually.

The automatic ways of building visualizations are fast and easy, but they are limiting. This is why you need to understand where to put the fields manually in order to create what you want.

# Building a visualization, the manual way

It's impossible to describe all the possibilities and combinations of how to build a visualization in Tableau. You are entirely free to choose where you want to use your fields. However, there are not many places to put them: here are the different options that you have:

- Put fields in **Rows** or **Columns**. If the pill is Discrete (blue), then you'll see a header. If the pill is Continuous (green), then you'll see an axis.

- Put fields in the **Marks** properties shelf (such as Color, Size, and Text).

- Add fields in **Filters**.
- Add fields in **Pages**.

That's it! With this, you can create every possible type of visualization in Tableau—there is no hidden menu and no secret page.

In the next section, you'll learn about the different Mark type with an example for each.

# The Mark type

The menu, highlighted in the following screenshot, allows you to choose the Mark type:

By default, the Mark type is set to **Automatic**. This means that Tableau chooses the best visualization based on the fields (that is, which data types you use and where).

Of course, you can change the Mark type and use any type you want. For example, if you put **Order Date** in **Columns** and **Profit** in **Rows**, Tableau displays a Line chart because it's the best way to visualize an evolution. However, by using the **Marks** shelf, you can select the one you prefer (for example, a bar chart, an area chart, or whatever you think is best).

Let's explore what you can build with the different Mark type. For almost every type, there is an example that you can reproduce with Sample - Superstore.

 You can also download the Mark Types ZIP file from my website (https://tableau2019.ladataviz.com) in *Chapter 6, Design Insightful Visualizations section*, or click on this direct link: http://ladataviz.com/wp-content/uploads/2019/05/ Mark-Types.zip. When you unzip the file, you'll find a Tableau Package Workbook with an example of each Mark type.

Let's start with our Mark type tour with bar charts:

- **Bar** ( 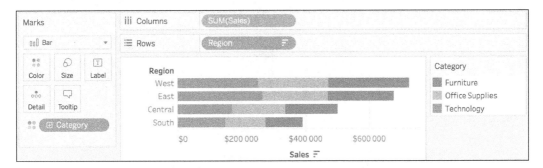 ): This is probably the most common and useful Mark type. It's perfect for comparing values between multiple categories. When you don't know how to visualize your data, start with a bar chart! Here's an example of a visualization using a bar chart:

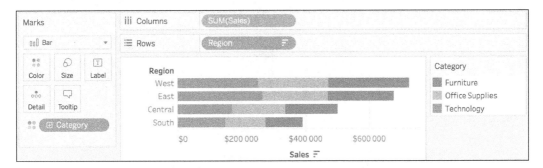

- **Line** ( $\sim$ ): This is useful for seeing trends and evolution. When you have multiple lines, you can easily compare the values at each time point. However, it's harder to see the global trend than with a bar. Here's an example of a visualization using a line chart:

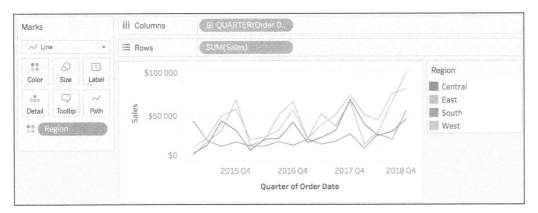

- **Area** (⌒): This is useful for seeing the global trend and the proportions at each time point. Here's an example visualization using an area chart:

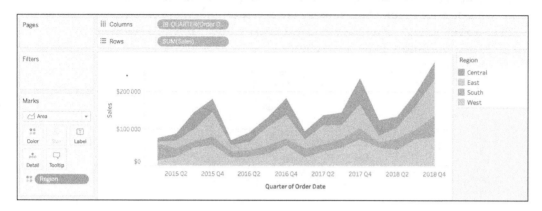

- **Square** (☐): You can create two types of charts with a square—a heatmap and a treemap. A heatmap is a table, but better. When you build a table, you have to read every value to compare them. A heatmap gives the same level of granularity, but with the ability to quickly spot the top and bottom values. Here's an example of a heatmap:

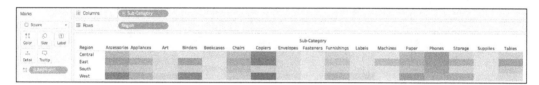

A treemap is a hierarchical representation, with nested rectangles, that gives you a quick idea of the number of values and the proportion of each of them. Here's an example of a treemap:

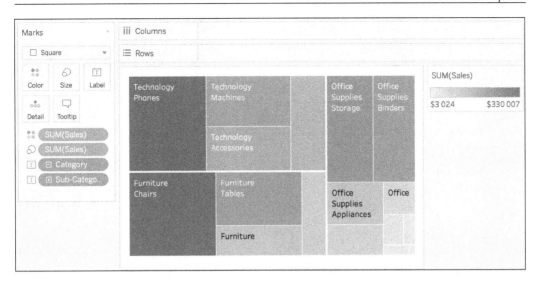

- **Circle** ( ○ ): The big advantage of this Mark type is that you can easily use two properties, Color and Size, on top of the position of the circle. In the following example, you can easily spot the biggest city, the sales, and the profit at a glance:

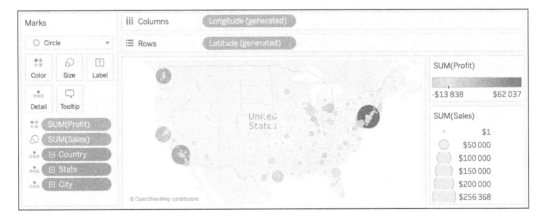

- **Shape** (⬚): When you use the shape Mark, the **Shape property** (the boxes beneath the Mark type menu) becomes available. To use a Shape, drag and drop a Dimension in the **Shape** property and each value gets a different shape. Here is an example of a visualization using Shape:

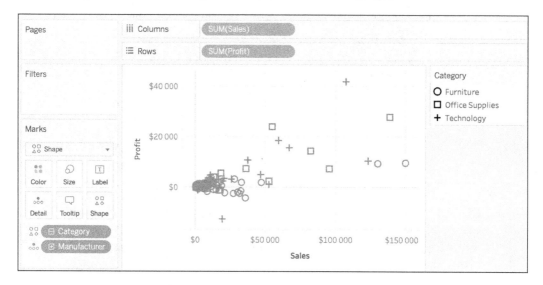

Wait, there's more! Shapes are among the best features to customize your visualization and create something unique. You can add any custom shapes you want in Tableau. You'll learn how to do that in the next section.

- **Text** ( T ): This is used to build tables but also word clouds. Tables will always be there. You can build the best visualization ever, but there will still be someone asking for a simple table because they need to see the values. You can't do anything about this, so you may as well learn how to create a table:

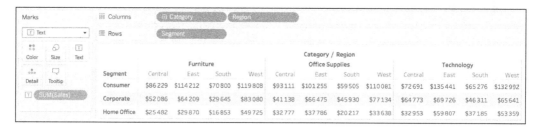

| | Category / Region | | | | | | | | | | | |
| | Furniture | | | | Office Supplies | | | | Technology | | | |
| Segment | Central | East | South | West | Central | East | South | West | Central | East | South | West |
| Consumer | $86 229 | $114 212 | $70 800 | $119 808 | $93 111 | $101 255 | $59 505 | $110 081 | $72 691 | $135 441 | $65 276 | $132 992 |
| Corporate | $52 086 | $64 209 | $29 645 | $83 080 | $41 138 | $66 475 | $45 930 | $77 134 | $64 773 | $69 726 | $46 311 | $65 641 |
| Home Office | $25 482 | $29 870 | $16 853 | $49 725 | $32 777 | $37 786 | $20 217 | $33 638 | $32 953 | $59 807 | $37 185 | $53 359 |

A word cloud isn't the best visualization to do an analysis. However, it can be used to see the big picture. As with circle, you can use a Measure in Size and another one in Color. Here's an example of a word cloud:

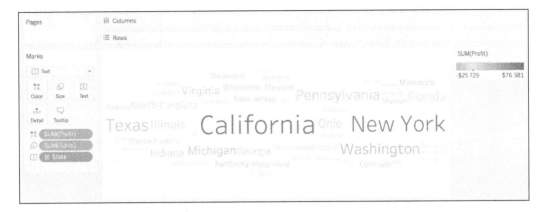

- **Map** ( ): To use the map Mark type, you need at least one Dimension with a geographical role in the **Marks** shelf, the **Longitude (generated)** field in **Columns**, and the **Latitude (generated)** field in **Rows**. When you display a map, there are options to search, zoom, and select values in the menu in the top-left corner of the map. Here's an example of a map in Tableau:

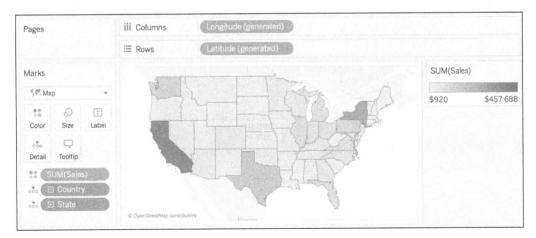

**Maps** are customizable. When you click on the **Map** top menu, you'll find options to change the background, use a custom geocoding, manually edit the locations, add the legend. However, the two most important options are:

- ° **Map layers**: Opens a new pane on the left where you can change the **Style** of the map, the **Washout**, and add or remove multiple **Layers** such as **Coastline**, **Cities**, **Country Borders**, **Building footprints**, and so on.

- ° **Map options**: Opens a new menu on the map where you can customize the options to search and zoom, but also change the units and remove the toolbar.

- **Pie** (⊙): When you select **Pie** in the **Mark type** selector, a new property becomes available: angle. To create a pie chart, put a Dimension in **Color** and a Measure in the **Angle** property. A pie chart works in one specific situation when you want to compare the proportion between two values. With more than two values, a bar chart is always more efficient. Here's an example of a visualization, representing the unranked sales by category with a pie chart and a bar chart:

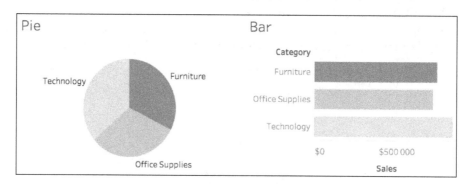

If you still want to create a pie chart, at least don't forget to sort the values as in the following example:

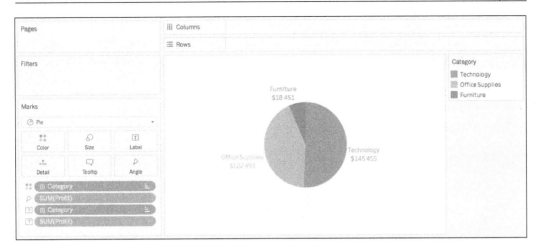

- **Gantt Bar** ( 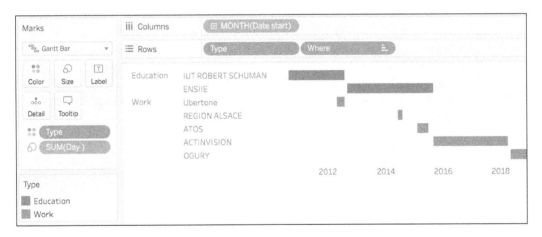 ): This is generally used to create a Gantt chart, and this visualization is helpful when you manage projects over time or if you want to create a timeline. A Gantt Bar uses a Continuous field (generally a date) in **Rows** or **Columns** to set the initial position and another Continuous field in **Size**. Here is an example of using a Gantt Bar for a resume:

- **Polygon** (  ): This Mark type exists when you want to represent something supposedly impossible to do in Tableau. When you select **Polygon**, a new property is available: Path. To create a polygon, you'll need a Dimension representing the unique identifier of each polygon, and a number in **Path** to connect the points and draw the polygons and coordinates in **Rows** and **Columns**. Once you have that, you can create, for example, the following polygon:

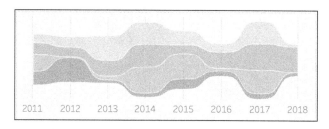

The preceding example is a Stream Graph created by Ludovic Tavernier. You can learn how to build a Stream Graph with this tutorial: `https://greatified.com/2018/09/17/how-to-build-a-stream-graph-in-tableau-software/`

- **Density** ( ⊙ ): The newest Mark type was introduced in Tableau 2018.3, and it allows you to show the density of your Marks. The superposition of multiple Marks determines the color intensity. It's a very simple Mark type; you can use it in various cases as long as you have many Marks overlapping. In the following example, you can see where the concentration of customers is by sales and quantity:

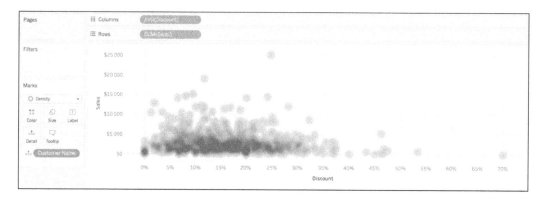

Now that you know how and when to use the different Mark type, it's time to learn how to use another critical part of the Marks shelf, that is, the Mark properties.

# Mark properties

There are five Mark properties that are always available: **Color**, **Size**, **Text/Label**, **Detail**, and **Tooltip**. There are also three properties available only when using a specific Mark type: **Shape**, **Path**, and **Angle**.

Any unaggregated field, returning more than one value that is used in a Mark property splits the number of Marks (except for the Tooltip property).

For example, if you put a Dimension that contains three different values in the Color property, the number of Marks is split by three.

Let's examine each property with the different options you have to make better visualizations. For each property, you'll find an example that you can reproduce with `Sample - Superstore` **and** `World Indicators`.

 You can also download the `Mark Properties` ZIP file from my website (`https://tableau2019.ladataviz.com`) in *Chapter 6, Design Insightful Visualizations*, or click on this direct link: `http://ladataviz.com/wp-content/uploads/2019/05/Mark-Properties.zip`. When you unzip the file, you'll find a Tableau Package Workbook with an example of each Mark type.

Let's start with the most frequently used property: Color.

# Color

Color is represented by the following icon: . It is probably the most useful and widely used property. It can be used to change the color of all the Marks, slice a Mark if you use a Dimension, or display another insight if you use a Measure.

If you don't place any fields on the Color property, then clicking on the **Color** button opens a menu where you can set the color of the Marks, change the opacity, and add borders and a halo. You can also click on **More colors...** to open a menu where you can choose the exact color of your choice. If you drag and drop a field on **Color**, Tableau uses colors to add a new layer of information. The behavior is different between a Continuous field and a Discrete field.

If you use a Discrete field (in blue and usually a Dimension), each value of the field has a distinct color. Tableau uses a default set of colors, but you can edit them by clicking on the **Color** button and then on **Edit Colors**.

A new window opens where you can choose between different color palettes and assign a specific color to each value. Here's an example of a Discrete field on **Color**, with the **Edit Colors** window:

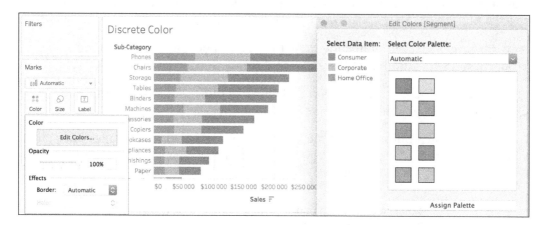

Additionally, on the **Edit Colors** window, to personalize your visualization even more, you can double-click on a data item to open another menu where you can choose any color of your choice. Using this menu, you can also use a color picker to select a color on your screen.

> It's possible to add a custom color palette by editing `Preference.tps` in your Tableau repository, as explained in the Tableau documentation at `https://onlinehelp.tableau.com/current/pro/desktop/en-us/formatting_create_custom_colors.html`.

If you use a Continuous field (in green and usually a Measure), Tableau uses a color gradient from the minimum value to the maximum value. If there are positive and negative values, Tableau automatically chooses a diverging palette. Again, the default color palette can be edited by clicking on the **Color** and **Edit Colors** options. If you edit the color of a Continuous Field, a different window opens. Here's an example of using a Continuous Field in Color with the Edit Colors window opened:

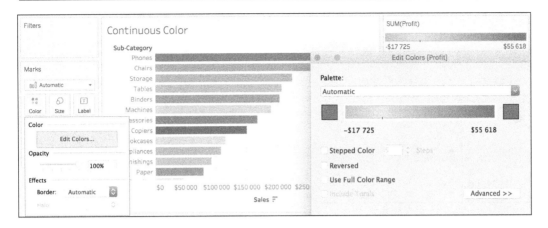

Using this menu, you have many options to configure your palette. You can set the number of steps, reverse the palette and, after clicking on the **Advanced** button, set the Start, Middle, and Center of the palette. Again, if you click on a color box, it opens an advanced menu to choose the exact color of your choice.

> When using the Density Mark type, you can modify the **Intensity** value by clicking on **Color**.

After Color, the second property is Size.

# Size

Size is represented by the following icon:  . Size is used almost all the time when designing a visualization. It can be used to simply change the size of the Marks or, as with Color, to add more information.

If you don't put any fields on the Size property, then clicking on the **Size** button opens a small menu where you can change the size of the Marks. If you put a field on the Size property, the values of the field will be represented with different sizes. If you use a Discrete field, each value has a specific size. If you use a Continuous field, Tableau uses a scale from the minimum value to the maximum value.

The following screenshot is an example of a Continuous field in **Size**:

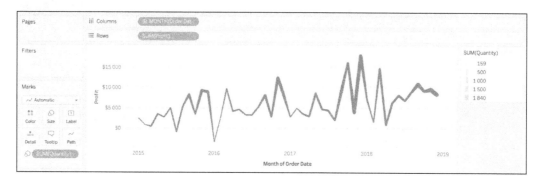

When using a field in the Size property, a legend appears (usually on the right-hand side). If you double-click on the legend, a new menu opens. Using this menu, you can choose how the size varies, but also set the Start, End, and Size range. Here is the menu:

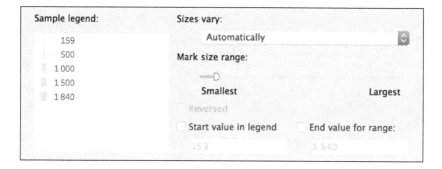

The next property reacts differently depending on the Mark type.

# Label (text)

Label (or text) is represented by this icon: [Label] . There are two different cases: when you use the **text** Mark type, and if you use any other type. In both cases, you can drag and drop multiple fields on the property.

If you use the text Mark type, this property is named **Text**. If you put a Measure in this property, the aggregated value is displayed. If you put a Dimension in this property, then all the different values are displayed, multiplying the number of Marks.

If you click on the **Text** button, you'll find an option to change the alignment and, if you click on the box with the three dots (**...**), Tableau opens the **Edit Label** window. This window is a text editor where you can modify the font, the size, the color, and write any text you want. Here's an example of **Sales** and **Quantity** in **Text** with the **Edit Label** window and the result:

If you use any Mark type other than text, then this property is named **Label** and you can use it to add a label to the current Marks (on a bar chart or a line chart, for example). The value of a Measure will be displayed in the visualization; a Dimension will split the number of Marks. When you click on the **Label** button, you'll find many options:

- **Show Mark labels** is the same as clicking on the ⊤ icon in the toolbar.

- The options under **Label Appearance** allow you to change the text, the font, and the alignment.

- The buttons under **Marks to Label** allows you to choose which Marks will have a label. You can add a label to all the Marks, to the maximum or minimum only, to only those that are selected, or to the highlighted ones.

- The last option allows the labels to overlap. By default, Tableau chooses to show the labels only if they don't overlap.

The following screenshot is an example of using a **Label** to add the **Profit Ratio**, **Segment**, and **Customer Name** information in **Circle**:

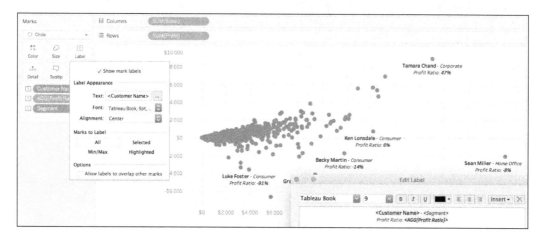

The next property is elementary, but also very useful!

# Detail

Detail is represented by this icon: . Like the previous Mark properties, dropping a Dimension on **Detail** splits the Marks. And that's it! This property does nothing more than splitting the Marks. You can use **Detail** to show your data at a less aggregated level.

Tooltip is the next property, and it's the only one that doesn't split the Marks.

# Tooltip

Tooltip is represented by this icon: .

The tooltip is displayed when you hover over a Mark. Any field that you drop on **Tooltip** is added to the tooltip box. The fields in the tooltip are always aggregated. For Dimensions, Tableau uses a special aggregation, ATTR, to display them. This aggregation returns the value if it's unique, otherwise, it shows *. Clicking on the **Tooltip** button opens a window where you can edit the text and change a few options.

Here's an example of a customized **Tooltip**:

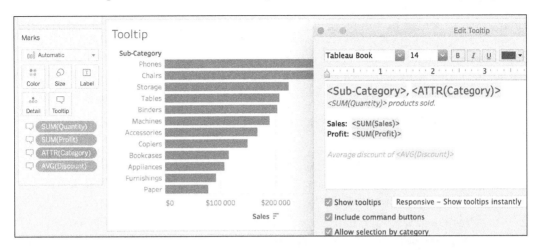

You can also add other Worksheets to the tooltip property. This functionality is called **Viz in Tooltip**. In the Tooltip editing window, in the top-left corner, you have the option to insert additional information but also other sheets. To learn more about this feature, you can visit `https://onlinehelp.tableau.com/current/pro/desktop/en-us/viz_in_tooltip.htm`.

Here is an example of a visualization using a Viz in Tooltip:

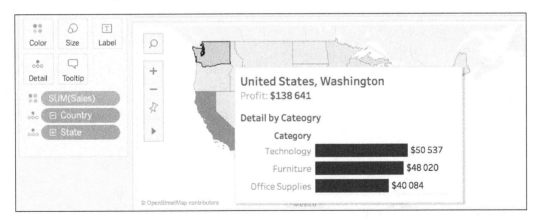

The next property, Shape, is only available with the Mark type of the same name.

# Shape

Shape is represented by this icon: 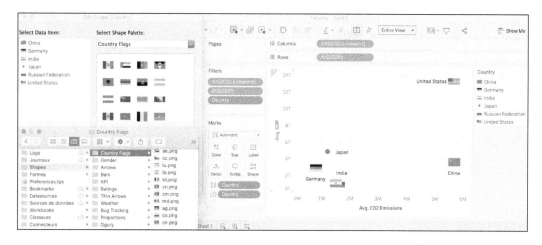 . You can only use a Discrete field with Shape. When you drop a field on the Shape property, the different values of the field are represented with different shapes. When you click on the **Shape** button, Tableau opens the **Edit Shape** window where you can, as with color, select predefined shape palettes and assign them to the values.

However, the really interesting aspect of shapes is that you can add **custom shapes**. You can do this as follows:

1. Find the `Shapes` folder in your **Tableau repository** (usually inside the `My Documents` folder on your computer). In the `Shape` folder, you'll find one folder for each shape palette.

2. Create a new folder, name it as you want, and put different images inside it (`PNG`, `JPG`, `BMP`, or `GIF` are accepted).

3. In Tableau, in the **Edit Shape** window, click on **Reload Shapes**, and you'll find your new palette with your custom shapes.

Here is an example of using country flags:

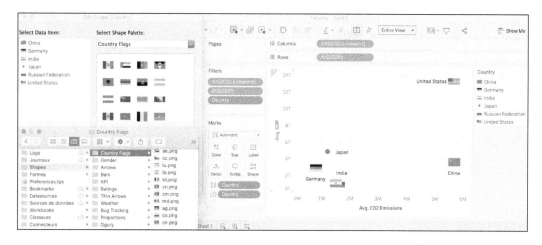

Next, let's see the Path property.

# Path

Path is represented by this icon: 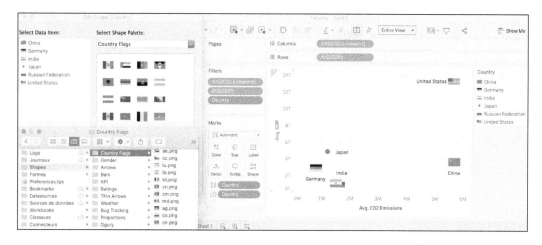 . This property is available for both line charts and polygons. If you click on the **Path** button, Tableau opens a menu where you can select the **Line Type**: **Linear**, **Step**, or **Jump**. Here's an example of a step line:

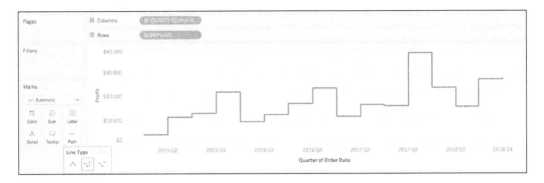

This property also allows you to choose the order to connect the Marks. Usually, you only use it if, in your data, there is a special order to connect the Marks to create a specific visualization as for polygons.

The next and final property only exists for pie charts.

# Angle

Angle is represented by this icon:  . You have to use an angle to create a pie chart and you can only use a Continuous field on **Angle**. When you use a field on **Angle**, the values are used to calculate the angle of the different portions of the pie.

You now have all the knowledge you need to build almost every visualization in Tableau, but to truly unleash Tableau's potential, you need to learn what you can do when using multiple Measures at the same time.

# Using multiple Measures

Until now, you've always used only one Continuous field (usually a Measure) at a time on the Rows or Columns shelf. Let's discover what happens when you use more than one.

If you use more than one Continuous field at a time in Rows or Columns, Tableau creates multiple axes, and the **Marks** shelf splits according to the number of Continuous fields (plus one for **All**). Each Marks shelf can have a different Mark type and properties.

> If you change the Mark type or properties for **All**, all the Marks are affected.

Let's build an example together, as follows:

1. Put the Continuous **Quarter** of **Order Date** in **Columns**, then **Profit** and **Profit Ratio** in **Rows**. The Marks shelf is split into three, one for **SUM(Profit)**, one for **AGG(Profit Ratio)**, and one for **All**, as you can see in the highlighted area:

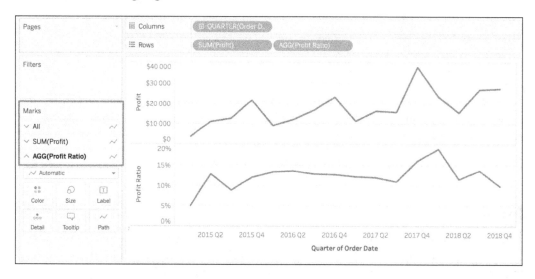

2. Click on the **SUM(Profit)** Marks shelf and change the Mark type to a **Bar** and the **Color** property to black as illustrated here:

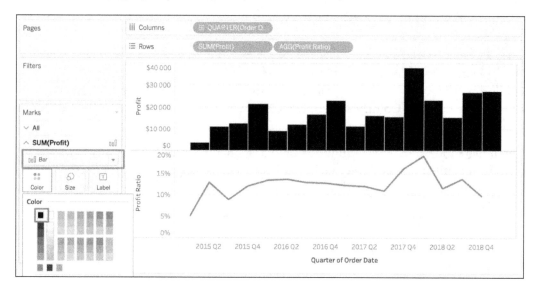

Keep this visualization for the next section!

As you can see, you can edit the different **Marks** shelves independently. But can we do more than that? Well, yes! Let's discuss dual axis and Measure values/names.

# Dual Axis

When you want to combine two Continuous fields, it is possible to create a dual axis. With a dual axis, there is one axis on the left, one on the right, and the Marks are superimposed. To create a dual axis, right-click on the **second** Continuous field and click on **Dual Axis**, as shown in the following screenshot:

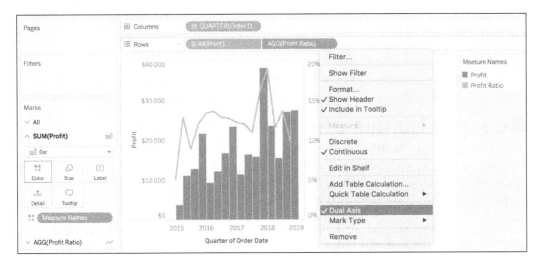

When using a dual axis, the **pills** are merged. If the Mark type is set to **Automatic**, they might change when using dual axis. However, it's still possible to edit them individually by using the different **Marks** shelves. By default, Tableau puts **Measure Names** in **Color** to distinguish the two fields. You can, of course, modify the color or remove it.

Dual Axis allows you to build new types of visualization, such as the following:

- **Donut chart**: `https://kb.tableau.com/articles/issue/creating-donut-charts`
- **Dual Axis map**: `https://onlinehelp.tableau.com/current/pro/desktop/en-us/maps_dualaxis.html`
- **Lollipop chart**: `https://www.tableau.com/fr-fr/about/blog/2017/1/viz-whiz-when-use-lollipop-chart-and-how-build-one-64267`

With dual axis, the range of the two different axes can be different. For example, in the preceding example, we compared the **Profit** in dollars and the **Profit Ratio** in percentages. However, if you're comparing values with a similar scale (such as sales from the current year and sales from the last year), the axes need to be in the same range. To do that, right-click on an axis and select **Synchronize Axis**.

But what if you need to compare more than two Measures? *Triple axis doesn't exist, sorry!* To do that, you'll use **Measure Names** and **Measure Values**.

## Measure Names and Measure Values

If you remember, in the data source, there is one special Dimension, **Measure Names**, and one special Measure, **Measure Values**. Measure values return the values of the different Measures and Measure Names return their names. You can use them to display as many Measures as you want.

When you use Measure values in View, Tableau displays the **Measure values** shelf where you can add as many Measures as you want.

The easiest way to display multiple Measures with Measure Values and Measure Names is to perform the following steps:

1. Put the Continuous Quarter of **Order Date** in **Columns** and **Sales** in **Rows**.

2. Drag and drop **Profit** over the existing axis (you can see the different icon when you're hovering above the axis), as shown in the following screenshot:

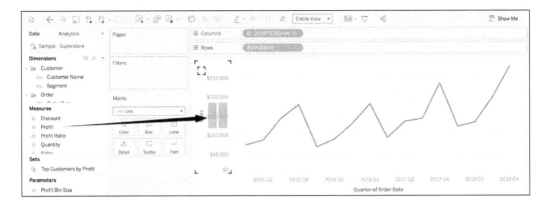

3. Tableau automatically replaces the **Sales** pill by **Measure Values**, puts **Measure Names** in **Color**, and also places it on the **Filters** shelf.

4. Now, you can add **Quantity** in the **Measure Values** shelf, as shown in the following screenshot:

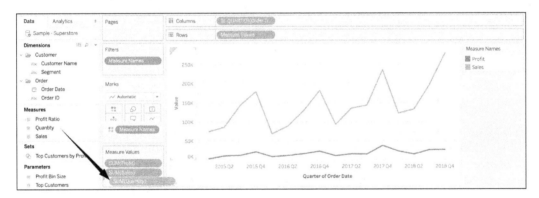

 Another way to add a new Measure is by editing the **Measure Names** filter and selecting the Measure you want.

5.  In contrast to Dual Axis, there is only one axis here, meaning that you can only have one scale. If the different Measures have significant different scales, it may be hard to see the variation. In the following screenshot, you can see that the **Quantity** values are too small, compared to **Sales** and **Profit**, to be readable:

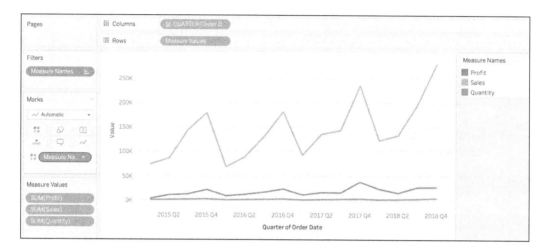

Another significant difference with a dual axis is that there is only one **Marks** shelf. That's because there is only one Continuous Field, **Measure Values**. This means that you cannot control the Mark type or properties for each Measure.

With Dual Axis, you can only combine two Continuous fields, but they can have different Mark types, properties, and axis ranges. With **Measure Values** and **Measure Names**, you can use as many Measures as you want, but only with one axis and one **Marks** shelf. The choice is yours, so use the best option!

The next section is unavoidable when speaking about data: Filters.

# Filters

Filtering a value is very simple in Tableau; you simply drag and drop any field onto the **Filters** shelf. You can filter as many fields as you want.

To decide where a filter should be applied, right-click on its pill in the **Filters** shelf, go to **Apply to Worksheets** and select one of the following options:

*   **All Using Related Data Sources**: Only useful when you have multiple data sources in your Workbook. This option allows you to filter on multiple data sources at the same time.

- **All Using This Data Source**: This option automatically adds the filter to every Worksheet that uses the current data source.
- **Selected Worksheets...**: This option opens a new window where you can manually select the different Worksheets where the filter should be applied.
- **Only This Worksheet**: The filter is only applied to the current Worksheet (by default).

Here's the menu:

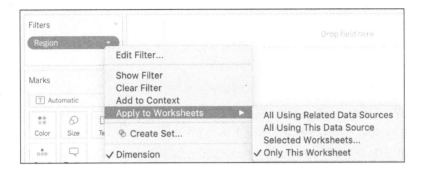

 If the field you want to filter is a Measure, a new window opens, asking you to choose an aggregation or **All values** (no aggregation).

There are differences between a Discrete and a Continuous field, and with dates compared to other data types. Let's discover those differences.

# Filtering a Continuous field

When filtering a Continuous field, Tableau opens the Continuous filters window. In this window, you have four options:

- **Range of values**: Select the minimum and maximum value; everything outside is excluded.
- **At least**: Select the minimum value; everything lower is excluded.
- **At most**: Select the maximum value; everything higher is excluded.
- **Special**: You can filter only the null or only the non-null values.

Let's discover what happens when you want to filter a Discrete field.

# Filtering a Discrete field

When you use a Discrete field on **Filters**, a new window automatically opens. In this window, you have four tabs with different options. The conditions you set on each tab are combined. Let's demonstrate how to use the different tabs:

- **General**: You can select the values you want to keep (or to exclude if you check the **Exclude** box). At the bottom, there are buttons to select **All** the values or **None**; at the top, you can choose between the following:
  - ° **Select from list**: This is the default option, where you can select each item.
  - ° **Custom value list**: This is where you can enter a list of custom values to keep or exclude.
  - ° **Use all**: To keep all the values.

- **Wildcard**: You can enter some text so that the filter keeps (or excludes) the values that **Contains**, **Starts with**, **Ends with**, or **Exactly matches** your text.

- **Condition**: You can specify a condition based on a field or formula. Only the values that fulfill the condition are kept.

- **Top**: This filter will only keep the values on top (or at the bottom) based on a value. There are four main drop-down menus to configure the filter:
  - ° Choose between either the **top** or **bottom** values
  - ° Specify the number of values to keep (with a number, a parameter, or, a set)
  - ° Select a field and an aggregation

Filters also allow you to add interactivity to your visualizations; this is possible thanks to **quick filters**.

# Quick filters

With a right-click on a pill in the **Filters** shelf, you can find the **Show Filter** option. It's the first option in this book that adds interactivity in Tableau. Clicking on **Show Filter** opens the **quick filter card** on the Worksheet.

 You can automatically add a quick filter by right-clicking on a field in the **Data** pane or a pill in **View** and selecting **Show Filter**.

The quick filter allows you, and the people who interact with the visualization, to filter the values without having to open a menu. Here's an example of a quick filter on **Region**, where only **Central** and **East** are selected:

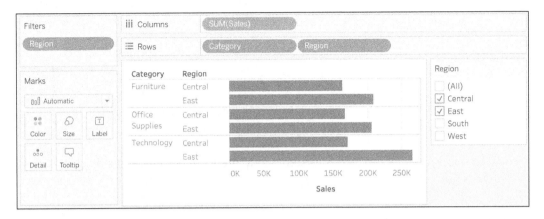

There are many interesting options when you click on the arrow in the top-right of the quick filter card:

Here's a selection of the most important options:

- You can allow **single** selections or **multiple** selections. For both options, you can choose between a **List**, a **Dropdown** list, or a **Slider**. The **Wildcard Match** is a bit different, as it allows any values to be entered and will keep the values that contain the pattern.

- In **Customize**, you can remove **all** from the quick filter list. It may be crucial that you don't allow all the values to be selected at once.

- In **Customize** again, the last option allows you to add an **Apply** button to the quick filters that allow multiple selections. It's useful when you have a long list of values, and you don't want the visualization to refresh after each selection.

- If you select **Only Relevant Values**, the quick filter only shows the possible values when considering the other filters. This option is similar to the **All Values in Hierarchy** option that is automatically applied when you are using fields from a common hierarchy. **All Values in Database** always shows all the values of the field, even if the combination of the different filters returns no lines.

> A quick filter based on a Continuous field is always represented by a slider. You can customize it to display the **Readouts**, the **Slider**, and the **Null** controls. You can also visually choose between the **Range of Values**, **At Least**, or **At Most**.

Now that you know how to add filters and play with quick filters, let's discuss the hierarchies between the filters.

# Filter hierarchy

All Dimension filters are applied at the same time. There is, by default, no hierarchy between them, but you can add one with **context**.

# Context

Using context is a way to add a hierarchy between the different Dimension filters. Consider the following example using Sample - Superstore:

1. Create a visualization with **City** in **Rows** and **Sales** in **Columns**, and use the button in the toolbar to sort the values.

2. Add **City** to the **Filters** shelf and, on the **Top** tab, select **Top** 5 **by Sales**, as shown in the following screenshot:

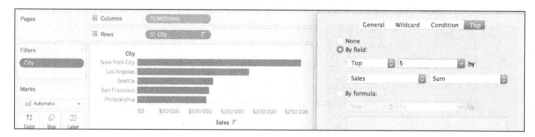

3. Add a quick filter to **State**. You can do this very easily with a right-click on the **State** field in the **Data** pane and selecting **Show Filter**.

4. In the quick filter, select only **California**. Tableau combines the two filters and looks for cities that are both in the global top five and in California. Tableau returns only two cities, **Los Angeles** and **San Francisco**. This is not what we want:

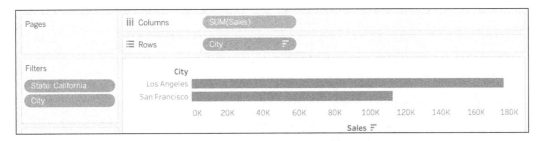

5. Right-click on the State pill on the **Filters** shelf and select **Add to Context**. The pill automatically turns gray and goes above the **City** pill. The result is as expected; you see the top five cities in California:

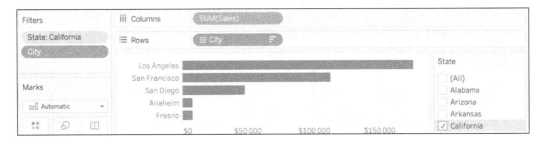

You can now select any state from the quick filter and see the top five cities in that state. Thanks to context, Tableau first filters the states and then keeps the top five cities.

Context is a great way to put hierarchies between your different filters. To end this section about filters, let's discuss the general hierarchies between different filters.

## Global filter hierarchy

There are six different types of filters that you can add. Some are stronger than others, and it's important to know the order in which the filters are applied. Always keep this book close to you when using Tableau, and look at the following screenshot if you need to ask yourself a question about the hierarchy between filters:

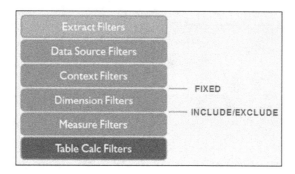

Of course, on top, you find **Extract Filters**. As the extract is a local copy of your data, if you add a filter when creating the extract, you completely remove the unwanted data from the data source. In second place, among the data source options, you can add **Data Source Filters**. All the data is present, but only some is used. Then, as we saw, **Context Filters** are stronger than the **Dimension Filters**. Finally, at the bottom, the last filters to be applied are the **Measure Filters**.

 Fixed, include/exclude, and table calculation are all advanced techniques, which we'll address later.

Let's continue with a very special shelf called **Pages**.

# Pages

Not only do pages add interactivity to your visualization, but they're also the only way to create animations in Tableau. You may have never seen a Tableau visualization with animations for a simple reason: Tableau Server and Tableau Public can't display the animations yet. But what exactly are pages?

 Pages are very rarely used because animations don't work when you publish your work. For this reason, we won't go into too much detail about this functionality.

Pages act as a single value filter. Each value is a page, and you can click on the **Play** button to go through all the pages and create an animation.

There are a few things to bear in mind if you want to use pages, as follows:

- You can only use Discrete fields in **pages**.
- When you put a field in **pages**, the pages card, displayed in the following screenshot, automatically opens:

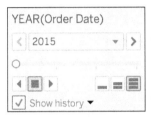

Here are some things you need to know about the page card:

- The first line displays the current page, and the arrows allow you to go to the next or previous value.
- The slider gives you an idea of how many values there are, and you can move the cursor to go through them.
- On the third line, on the left-hand side, you can see the animation buttons. You can use them to automatically go through all the pages or to stop the animation. On the same line, on the right-hand side, you can see the speed buttons. They define how fast Tableau changes the page.
- At the bottom, you can decide whether to show the history.

If you decide to **Show history**, a new menu opens.

In this menu, you can configure how to display the Marks from the preceding pages. Let's briefly explore the different options if you decide to show the history:

- In the first part, you specify which Marks should display the history (for example, only the one you selected or all).
- In the second part, you define how many historical Marks to show (for example, all or the last number of your choice).
- The third part allows you to choose between showing the historical Marks, only the trails (that is, the path from the prior point to the next), or both.
- Finally, in the two other parts, you can customize the format of the historical Marks or the trails.

For more example about animations and pages, visit `https://onlinehelp.tableau.com/current/pro/desktop/en-us/buildmanual_shelves.htm#pages-shelf`.

We have seen all the different shelves available in Tableau. To conclude this chapter, let's take a look at the various options that are available in a Worksheet.

# Worksheet options and formats

There are lots of options available in a Worksheet, and you can find them in many different places. The three most usual places to find options are as follows:

- With a right-click on a pill
- In the **Worksheet** menu at the top
- By right-clicking on the **View** (or on a **Mark**)

Let's go through a selection of the most useful options for each place, starting with the pill options.

# Pill options

Many options are available by right-clicking on a pill. As always, there are some differences between Continuous and Discrete pills.

Among the most important options, you'll find the following:

- **Filter...**: A shortcut to put the current pill in the **Filters** shelf and open the **Edit Filter** window.
- **Show Filter**: This automatically puts the pill in the Filters shelf and displays the quick filter (it doesn't open the menu).
- **Show Highlighter** (only for Discrete pills): This opens the **Highlighter** card, which allows you to highlight a specific value, as shown in the following screenshot:

- **Sort** (only for Discrete pills): This opens the **Sort** window, where you can change the sort order of the values.

You can also directly transform the pill into a **Dimension**, an **Attribute**, or a **Measure**. If the pill returns a number, you can choose between converting it to **Discrete** or **Continuous**. If the pill is a Measure, then you can also create table calculations, but that's for another chapter!

Next, we'll see the options available on the Worksheet menu.

# Worksheet menu options

At the top, among the different menus of Tableau, you can find the **Worksheet** menu, which contains a few interesting options. Again, let's focus on the more important ones, as follows:

- **Export** allows you to export the Worksheet as an **image**, as **data** (a CSV file), or an **Excel cross-tab**. If you choose image, a new window opens where you can customize the result. The **Data** and **Excel** options both convert the visualization into a table.

- **Tooltip...** is a shortcut to edit the tooltip.

- With the different **Show...** options, you can display or hide many different shelves or cards as well as the sort controls. The **Caption** is a quick description of the Worksheet, and the Summary adds statistical information to the visualization.

- **Duplicate as Crosstab** duplicates your current Worksheet to create a new one and transforms the visualization into a table.

> By right-clicking in the bottom of the Worksheet tab, you can perform the same action.

The final sets of options are available with a right-click on the **View**.

# View options

In case you forgot, the part that displays the visualization and contains the headers, axes, and Marks is called the **View**. When you right-click on the different elements of the View, you may find a number of attractive options.

As before, you'll find here a list and description of the most useful options:

- **View Data** opens a new window with, by default, a **summary** of the displayed data, or the **full data**, which shows all the lines that are used to build the visualization. From the **View Data** window, you can also **copy** or **export** the current selection to a CSV file.

- **Edit Locations...** is available when the Mark has a geographical role and lets you configure the locations in a new window.

- With **Mark Label**, you can force the Mark to always, or never, show the label.

- **Annotate** lets you add an annotation to a specific **Mark**, **Point**, or **Area** in the View. When you select one of the three options, Tableau opens the **Edit Annotation** window, where you can customize the text. Adding an annotation is an excellent way to add context to your visualization. Here's an example of an annotation:

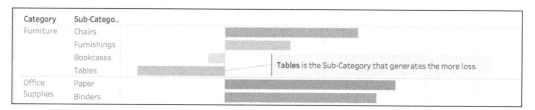

- **Keep Only** and **Exclude** are options that are available with a simple left-click on a Mark. **Keep Only** automatically adds a filter that includes only the value of the selected Mark. **Exclude** also adds a filter, but this time, the filter excludes the selected value. Both options can be handy for focusing on the interesting values and eliminating mistakes in your data.

If you right-click on an axis, you can edit it. Tableau opens the **Edit Axis** window, where you can configure many aspects of the axis, such as the range, the scale, the titles, and the tick Marks.

Always remember that if you are searching for how to configure or edit something in Tableau, a simple right-click is almost always enough. This is the case, for example, for opening a very useful final option: format.

# Format

When you select the **Format** options, Tableau opens a whole new pane on the left-hand side rather than the **Data** pane. The formatting pane is highlighted in the following screenshot:

There are five different icons for the various formatting options available. For each option, the formatting can be applied to the Worksheet, the **Rows**, or the **Columns**, and to different parts of the View (**Worksheet, Pane, Header, Title**, and so on). The five formatting options allow you to do the following:

- **Format Font**: Select the font type, size, and color
- **Format Alignment**: Change the text alignment, direction, and wrapping
- **Format Shading**: Add a background color, and column or row banding
- **Format Borders**: Add a border and column or row dividers
- **Format Lines**: Change the format (to plain or dotted) of the different lines in Tableau (such as grid lines, zero lines, trends lines, and more)

> There is also an entire **Format** menu on top, where you can change the format of almost everything in Tableau. In this menu, you can open the **Format Workbook** pane, which is very useful for configuring the format of the entire Workbook in a few clicks.

With those options, you can quickly make everything beautiful or ugly. The only advice I can give you on this is to keep it simple, readable, and easy to understand!

# Summary

You now have all the keys to build your first visualizations, automatically or manually. The different Mark types and properties no longer hold any mystery for you. You also learned how to build a visualization with more than two Measures using Dual Axis, Measure Names, and Measure Values.

In this chapter, you also learned how to use filters to focus on the right data. Then, we looked at pages and how to add interactivity to Tableau! To finish, we explored the most useful options, where to find them, and how to use them.

This chapter is the longest and most important one in the book. It's the core of Tableau and where you'll spend a major part of your time. I'm sure you'll enjoy building many different visualizations to find the ones that make your data shine.

Once you find the best visualizations to understand your data and answer your questions, it's time to assemble them in a Dashboard. You have probably already guessed where this is going - the next chapter is about building Dashboards, how to create them and make them interactive, and, of course, this will be a chapter containing all the best advice and lots of examples.

# 7
# Powerful Dashboards, Stories, and Actions

A Dashboard is a composition of multiple Worksheets, and objects such as Container, Text, Image, and Actions to create interactivity. The goal of a Dashboard is to provide insights on a regular basis. The look and feel don't change, just the data. In this chapter, you'll learn how to create a Dashboard, you'll understand the different objects available, and will be able to choose between the different Actions. A Story is a composition of Worksheets and Dashboards. You'll learn how to create and use a Story to do a presentation, or to tell an amazing story you found in your data.

In this chapter, we'll cover the following topics:

- Dashboard basics
- Dashboard objects
- Dashboard actions
- Creating a Story

Let's start with the Dashboard basics.

## Dashboard basics

If a Worksheet is one idea, a Dashboard is a way to combine multiple such ideas. With a Dashboard, you can create interaction between the Worksheets, and add pictures, web pages, and other objects to create a unique page that will answer all your questions.

To add a new Dashboard, you can either click on the icon at the bottom-right, ⊞, , click on **New Dashboard** from the **Dashboard** top menu, or use the **New Dashboard** button in the toolbar.

The Dashboard workplace is composed of a central blank part where you can drop Worksheets and objects. On the left pane, you can find two tabs, **Dashboard** and **Layout**:

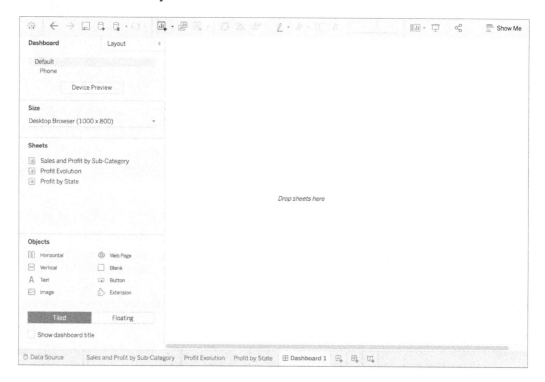

 You can't see the **Data** pane when creating a Dashboard. If you need to modify your data source, you have to go to a Worksheet.

Let's start by seeing how to build a Dashboard; then, we'll focus on the two different tabs.

# Building a dashboard

To create a Dashboard, you have to drag Worksheets or objects to the central blank area (you can also double-click on a Worksheet, but as always, you let Tableau build it for you).

A Worksheet that you add in a Dashboard is the Worksheet itself; this means that if you modify the Worksheet, you'll see the change in both the Dashboard and the Worksheet.

Usually, the purpose of a Worksheet is to end up in a Dashboard. You can hide all the Worksheets that are in a Dashboard by using the **Hide All Sheets** option when you right-click on a **Dashboard** tab. You can, of course, unhide them as easily.

You cannot modify any of the Worksheet shelves from the Dashboard. However, you can still use all the toolbar buttons (to sort, add labels, swap, create groups, and so on) and use a right-click to change the format, or all the other options we've seen in the previous chapter.

When you click on a Worksheet in a Dashboard, its outline will turn gray, and you'll see four (or five) icons:

- ☒: The first removes the Worksheet from the Dashboard.

- ☑: The second takes you to the Worksheet to modify it.

- ▽: The third is a shortcut to put a filter action on the Worksheet (detailed in a later section).

- ⬛: The fourth icon is optional, and it can be used to fix the width or height of the Worksheet if it's inside a horizontal or vertical Container.

- ▼: The last one, the small arrow, opens the options for the selection Worksheet. Many of those options can be found elsewhere among the Worksheets or Dashboard options. The most useful options are probably legends, Filters, and parameters, which allow you to quickly add the Legends, Filters, or Parameters that exist on the Worksheet to the Dashboard.

Speaking of options, let's discover what you can do with the pane on the left.

# The dashboard and layout panes

On the left of the Dashboard workplace, you can find two panes, **Dashboard** and **Layout**. Simply click on **Dashboard** or **Layout** to open the different panes.

## The Dashboard pane

On the top, you'll find the different device layouts available for your Dashboard. You'll learn more about that in a later section of this chapter.

The second—and more important than you think—useful option is **Size**. Here, you can set the size of your Dashboard to **Fixed** (with a list of standard sizes, and also the option to set the height and width manually), **Automatic** (the Dashboard will resize to fit the screen), or **Range**, with a minimum and maximum range.

**Automatic** may seem to be the best option, but it is often the worst. The ratio between height and width is critical in data visualization, and with automatic sizing, you have no control. A bad ratio can lead your Dashboard to look very bad, even unusable. My advice is to go with **Fixed** size when you want absolute power over the looks of your visualization, or choose **Range** to allow resizing for when the Dashboard will be displayed on many different screen sizes.

On the **Dashboard** pane, the part you'll use the most is sheets. Here, you'll find all the different Worksheets in your workbook, as long as they are not hidden (you understand, now, why giving a meaningful name to each of them is crucial).

Beneath the list of Worksheets, you can find the different objects that you can add to your Dashboard, and the option to choose between **Tiled** and **Floating**. All these essential functionalities will be seen in detail in this chapter.

To finish, at the very bottom, you can use the checkbox to choose whether to show the Dashboard title. Let's continue on to the Layout pane.

# The Layout pane

The Layout pane is handy when you select a Worksheet or Container in the Dashboard. You can show or hide its title, make it float or not, change its position and size (only for floating items), add a border, modify the background, and add outer and inner padding. Don't be afraid to try those different options, especially the padding, to add some space to your Dashboard.

At the bottom, you'll find the **Item hierarchy**:

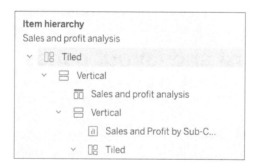

Here, you can unfold all your Dashboard items to find, edit or remove them. Among the different elements, you'll see the added Worksheets, but also the different Dashboard objects. Since Tableau Desktop 2019.1, you can rename the different Containers.

Now, let's explore the difference between Tiled and Floating.

# Tiled or floating layouts

When you drag and drop a Worksheet or an object on your Dashboard, you can either use **Tiled** or **Floating** layouts. Some users don't like Tiled; others consider Floating dangerous. Let's see the pros and cons.

## Tiled

Tiled is the default way to add elements on a Dashboard. At the beginning, it seems perfect: the grey part where you're dragging an element helps you to see where it'll go; the different items are distributed evenly; and it stays in place when you resize the Dashboard. But rapidly, you'll notice the limits of that technique.

Many cons make it hard to create a great Dashboard with Tiled Layouts:

- You have low control over the size and position of the elements.
- Achieving a pixel-perfect Dashboard is a big fight (maybe a little less now that the grid exists).
- You cannot add a border or a background that outlines multiple items.
- You cannot move multiple items at the same time.

What about the Floating Layout, then?

## Floating

The Floating Layout often became the default layout for people who had terrible experiences with Tiled. With this layout, you can drag and drop any element wherever you want. With the **Layout** pane, you can define the exact position and size of every item. Among the options (with the small descending arrow), you can also specify the Floating order to move the element to the back or the front.

The Floating Layout seems to be far better than Tiled, but it's more time-consuming to define the position and size of everything on the Dashboard. Also, the main problem is the time you have to spend if you need to make changes in your Dashboard. Let's say that you want to add a new Worksheet above all the existing ones—you'll need to reset the position and size of all the existing elements on your Dashboard, one by one. That's also the case when you resize the Dashboard.

In short, Tiled is probably better for quick business dashboards that can easily evolve, and Floating is better for pixel-perfect one pagers. Fortunately, there is a third solution, using Containers, that we'll see in the next section about objects. But first, let's talk about device layouts.

# Device layouts

You can create different device layouts on your Dashboard. Then, depending on the device used to open the Workbook (on Tableau Public, Server, or Mobile), the right layout is automatically chosen.

Since Tableau 2019.1, every Dashboard starts with two layouts: the default layout that you use to build your Dashboard, and an automatic **Phone** layout generated by Tableau.

To visualize or add new device layouts, click on the **Device Preview** button on the **Dashboard** pane to open the layout toolbar:

On this toolbar, you can select the type of device, the model, and the orientation of the layout. When you're done, click on the last button to add the layout and start personalizing it. You can add two additional layouts: **Desktop** and **Tablet**.

On the Dashboard pane on the left, you can click on the different layouts to switch from one to the other and configure them. You can specify the fitting and the height of the layout. You can also see the different items that exists in the **Default** layout and choose to keep or remove them (they are only removed from the selected layout and not from the other layouts). It's also possible to add other objects, such as text, that will be visible only for the selected layout.

Since Tableau Desktop 2019.1, you have two options for the **Phone** layout: either use the automatic layout generated by Tableau, or edit it manually.

Let's finish this introduction with the different Dashboard options.

# Dashboard options

In the top menu, between **Worksheet** and **Story**, you can find the different **Dashboard** options.

Among those options, the most important one surely is **Actions....** There is a focus on Actions in a later section. Format is also handy as you can configure the Dashboard color background, titles, and text objects.

The **Grid** is a great feature if, like me, you like when everything is properly aligned. You can decide whether to show the Grid, and how to configure its size.

To show or hide the Grid, you can also press the *G* key on your keyboard!

All the other options are either straightforward to understand and use (such as **Export Image...**) or just duplicates of options in different places (such as **Device Layouts**, **Show Title**, and **Auto Update**).

That's it for the basics, but you still have many things to learn about Dashboards! A major part of building a Dashboard is adding objects.

# Dashboard objects

Most of the objects are very simple. Drag and drop them on the Dashboard to use them. Here's a list of existing objects:

- **Text**: Drag and drop a Text object anywhere in your Dashboard and you'll be able to add free text. This is great for titles, explanations, credits, and so on.

- **Image**: This is the same as Text, except you'll add an image instead of text. You can add almost any image files. This is great for logos or to add some context to your Dashboard. Once you've added an image, you have a few options when you right-click on it, such as fit or center the image, or add a target URL when someone clicks on the picture.

- **Web Page**: This is more useful than you think! Of course, you can use it to display a web page in your Dashboard, but you can also link this web page to a Dashboard action to load different URLs based on your data. We will look at this in more detail in the *Go to URL action* section.

- **Blank**: Inserts a blank space.

- **Extensions**: A recent feature that enables you to add new features or interact with data from other applications. When you add an extension to your Dashboard, a new window opens asking to select a .trex file. You can either create your own extensions, or download one from the Extension gallery at https://extensiongallery.tableau.com/.

 If you want to learn how to build your own extensions, you'll find tutorials, samples, and clear explanations on the Tableau Extensions GitHub page, at https://tableau.github.io/extensions-api.

Each extension has its own permissions and configuration window.

- **Button**: Another recent feature to navigate between your Dashboards or Worksheets—it adds a button that you can, with a right-click, configure (to specify where to navigate) and personalize (change the image or add a tooltip).

As you can see, most of the objects are easy to understand and use. However, there are two other objects, the containers, that need a bit more explanation.

# Containers

The purpose of a Container is to group elements inside a shared space and allow you to have better control over those elements inside. They can be horizontal or vertical. The following screenshots are an example of three worksheets in a horizontal container:

 You can recognize a container by the blue dotted lines between the Worksheets.

When you add a Container, it'll be empty. Then, you can drag and drop Worksheets or objects inside it. You can also add another Container inside a Container, and so on; it's a good practice that I advise you to adopt. The first thing you do when you start to build a Dashboard should be adding a container.

If you have Containers inside Containers, you can select the parent Container by clicking on **Select Layout Container** among the options (available with a click on the small arrow from a select element), or you can also simply double-click on the grip part of every element, as highlighted in the following screenshot:

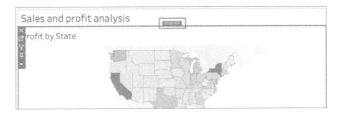

[  Another way to select a specific Container is to use the **Item hierarchy** in the Layout pane. ]

Containers act like the other elements in a Dashboard. The only difference is that their outline is blue when selected (while the other items are grey).

So, why exactly are Containers a good solution? First, every element inside a Container has two great options:

- **Fix Width** for a horizontal Container or **Fix Height** for a vertical Container. If this option is ticked, the width/height of the element will not change. So, if you change the size of your Dashboard or add new elements, the size of the fixed item won't move.

[ In a Container, you should always have at least one element whose width/height is not fixed, so it can fill the space or shrink. ]

- **Edit Width...** for a horizontal Container or **Edit Height...** for a vertical Container. This option allows you to set a specific width/height, in pixels, for every element inside the Container. Did you want pixel-perfect options as you had with the Floating Layout? You've got it!

The second reason is that among the Container options, you'll find **Distribute Evenly**, which you can see in the following screenshot:

If you select this option, every element inside the Container will have the same width (or height, depending on the Container type) and will resize if you add another item and change the size of the Dashboard.

With Containers, you can set the size of any element to the last pixels or distribute them evenly. By adding Containers into Containers, you can use all those features at the same time.

Let's continue to explore the uses of Dashboard and add a bit of Action!

# Dashboard actions

Actions are the more common and easiest way to add interactivity in Tableau. Usually, you'll add an action to create interactivity between the different Worksheets of your Dashboard, but you can also add an action that modifies the Worksheet itself. Actions have at least one Worksheet as a source, and a target that depends on the Action type.

There are three ways to trigger an Action:

- **Hover**: Just put your mouse over a mark, and the action is triggered.
- **Select**: The action is triggered when you click on a mark.
- **Menu**: A link is added at the bottom of the tooltip when clicking on a mark, but the action is only triggered if you click on that link. The text of the link can be customized.

You'll find the option to add an action in the Dashboard or Worksheet top menu. When you click on **Actions...**, a new window opens where you can add different types of actions, as you can see in the following screenshot:

There six different Actions: **Filter...**, **Highlight...**, **Go to URL...**, **Go to Sheet...**, **Change Parameter...**, and **Change Set Values...**.

 You can download a ZIP file called `Actions` from the **Chapter 7: Create Powerful Dashboards and Stories** section of my website, `https://tableau2019.ladataviz.com` (or, browse to `http://ladataviz.com/wp-content/uploads/2019/05/Actions.zip`). When you unzip the file, you'll find a Tableau Package Workbook that contains an example for each action.

Let's now look at the different types of Actions, starting with the most common one: Filter.

# The Filter action

The Filter action is the most common. From one or multiple Source Worksheets, you can filter one or numerous target worksheets. It's the only Action with a quick shortcut: when you select a Worksheet, click on the funnel icon, **Use as Filter**, and a Filter Action is automatically generated with the selected Worksheet as Source and all the others as targets. Of course, if you need more configuration, you'll need to add it from the **Action...** menu.

The next screenshot is an example of a Filter action where the selection of a US state filters the **Sales and Profit by Sub-category** worksheets in that state:

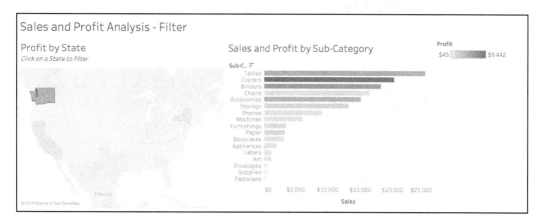

With the Filter action menu, you can specify exactly which fields need to be filtered. You can also dictate the behavior when clearing the Action. There are three different behaviors:

- **Leave the filter**: When you clear the selection, the Filter stays as it is. It's the default option for the Menu trigger.

- **Show all values**: When you clear the selection, you'll see all the values. It's the default option for the **Select** or **Hover** trigger.

- **Exclude all values**: When you clear the selection, the target Worksheets turn blank, as all values have been excluded. It's only when you trigger the Action again that the selected data is included.

The Target Worksheets can be in another Dashboard. Then, when you trigger the Action, you'll be automatically redirected to that Dashboard.

The next Action is **Highlight**. It's a great way to help the users understand the related fields in your Dashboard.

# The Highlight action

The Highlight action is also used quite often. From one or multiple Source Worksheets, you can highlight fields on one or multiple Target Worksheets. The next screenshot is an example of a Highlight action, where hovering over a category from one of the two bottom Worksheets automatically highlights it on both visualizations:

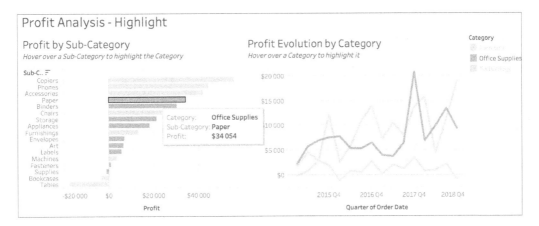

In the preceding screenshot, we hovered over an **Office Supplies** category in the **Profit Evolution by Sub-Category** Worksheet. Thanks to the Highlight Action, we can easily spot this category on the Profit by Category Worksheet.

As for the Action filter, you can specify in the configuration window which fields should be highlighted.

 Contrary to the Action filter, the fields that you want to highlight need to exist in both the Source and the Target Worksheets (no matter where; it can be in the Detail Mark property, for example).

The next Action, **Go to URL...**, is a great way to add interaction with the world outside of Tableau.

# The Go to URL action

The **Go to URL...** action allows you to open a website directly inside the Dashboard or in a new window.

The following screenshot is an example of a Go to URL... action where, when you click on a state in the map, a menu opens saying **Open State Wikipedia** page, and if you click on the link, the Wikipedia page of the state opens on the right, in a Web Page object:

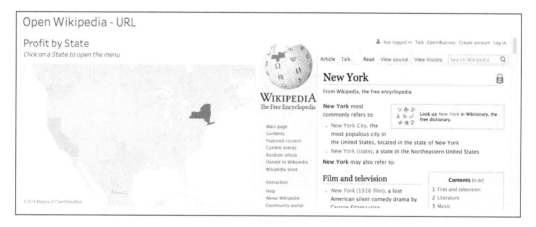

In the configuration window, you have to specify the URL of the web page you want to reach. You can write any URL you want, and, thanks to the small arrow at the end, add fields from the Worksheet. In the example, we wrote `https://en.wikipedia.org/wiki/` and we added the `State` field at the end. You can use the **Test Link** button to verify that your URL is working.

Since version 2019.2, you have the ability to choose how to open the URL target:

- **New Browser Tab**: Always opens the link in a new browser tab, even if a Web Page object exists in the Dashboard.
- **Web Page Object**: Opens the URL in a Web Page object in your Dashboard. You can even have multiple Web Page objects in you Dashboard with multiple URL actions targeting each Web Page object distinctly.
- **Browser Tab if No Web Page Objects Exists**: The default option – it opens the URL in a browser tab if there is no Web Page object.

Let's continue with the *Go to Sheet... action.*

# The Go to Sheet action

The Go to Sheet... action is very simple. From one or multiple source Worksheets, you can navigate to a target Worksheet or Dashboard. This action is quite similar to the button object, but with the possibility to add a navigation action on Worksheets.

The next action allows you to play with Parameter!

# The Change Parameter action

Change Parameter... is the newest action introduced in Tableau 2019.2. It allows you to visually change the value of a parameter based on a Worksheet. Previously, you had to change it from a menu.

 You'll learn more about parameters in *Chapter 10, Analytics and Parameters.*

The following screenshot is an example of how to use this new Action. When you hover over a State, it updates the value of a parameter based on the sales of the hovered state. This parameter is used as the point of comparison against the other states. With that, you can very easily find the states with higher or lower sales than the one you focus on (**Washington** in the following example):

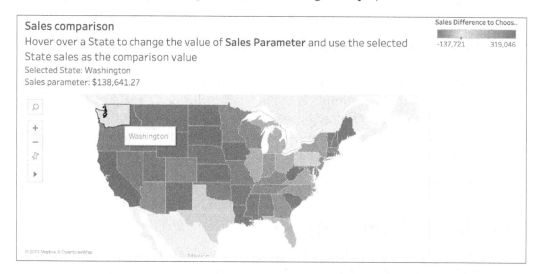

The configuration window for this action is quite straightforward: you select the source Worksheet(s), the trigger, the target parameter, and the field used to update the value of the parameter. As for the highlight action, the field you want to use to update the parameter needs to be in the view.

This new action will unlock many new opportunities to create awesome interaction for the users. Another recent action that opened many new possibilities is the **Change Set Values...** action.

# The Change Set Values action

The **Change Set Values...** action allows you to select, visually, the values to put in a set. The behavior is quite similar the **Change Parameter...** action. One of the biggest differences is that a parameter can only have one value, whereas sets can have multiple values in them.

In the next example, you can see the usage of the **Change Set...** action to drill down from the **Furniture** category to display its sub-categories:

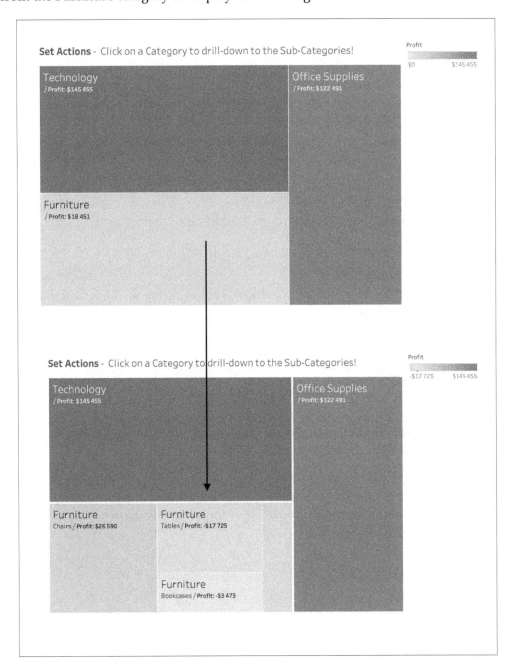

When you create a **Change Set Values...** action, in the configuration window, you can specify source Worksheets, the trigger, the data source, and the set that will be impacted by the action. As a set is based on a field, this field needs to be on a Worksheet.

As for the action filter, you can dictate the behavior when clearing the action. There are three different behaviors:

- **Keep set value**: When you clear the selection, the current values of the set stay as selected.

- **Add all values to set**: When you clear the selection, all the values are added to the set.

- **Remove all values from set**: When you clear the selection, all the values will be removed out of the set.

That's it for Actions. In the next section, we'll see how to create a Story.

# Creating a story

Stories are designed for data storytelling. You can control what the users will discover, in which order, and add annotations and explanations throughout the Story.

 Do not create a Story just to use it as a menu to navigate around the Dashboard. For that, you have the button object and the **Go to Sheet...** action.

Creating a new Story is as simple as creating a Dashboard; you can either click on the icon at the bottom-right, click on **New Story** from the Story top menu, or use the **New Story** button in the toolbar.

The Story workplace is quite similar to the Dashboard one. You'll find a central blank part where you can drop Worksheets and Dashboards. Again, modifying the Dashboards or Worksheets will impact the Story. On the left pane, you can also find two tabs: **Story** and **Layout**.

The main difference with Dashboards is the **Story points**. A Story is usually composed of multiple Story points. Each of them can contain only one Worksheet or one Dashboard. Here's an example of three Story points:

When you hover over a Story point, you'll see these four icons:

Each icon has a unique function:

- The first one removes the Story point
- The second icon reverts the changes to the latest updated state
- The third one refreshes the Story point and memorizes the changes in a new state
- The last icon saves the current changes in a new Story point

Now that we've seen the basics, let's start to create a Story.

# Building a story

You begin to build a Story in a Story point. Each Story point contains one Worksheet or one Dashboard. You can add them with a simple drag-and-drop to the central blank area (or use a double-click). Then, you can create a new blank Story point and add another Sheet or duplicate the existing one to Highlight or Filter a specific element. The Story keeps the selection, Highlights, and Filter added on each Story point.

We will now create a Story together. To reproduce the example, download the ZIP file, `Story Start`, from the **Chapter 7: Create Powerful Dashboards and Stories** section of my website, `https://tableau2019.ladataviz.com` (or, browse to `https://ladataviz.com/wp-content/uploads/2019/05/Story-Start.zip`).

When you unzip the file, you'll find a Tableau Package Workbook that contains a Dashboard you already built earlier (with a Filter action when you click on the map):

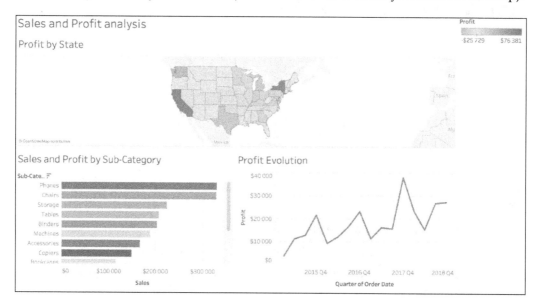

Let's start building our first story:

1. Create a new Story and call it `Sales and Profit Insights`.

2. Drag and drop the **Sales and Profit Analysis** Dashboard in the Story, and change the caption of the Story point to `Sales and Profit Analysis`.

3. Duplicate the current Story point with the button on the left.

4. On this new Story point, click on the State of Texas, change the caption to `Texas is the less profitable State`, and click on the **Update** button in the Story point to save the changes. Here is how your Story should look, and where to find the button to update:

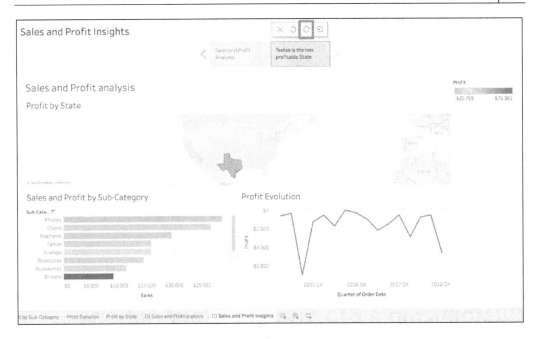

5. On the `Texas is the less profitable State` Story point, click on the State of California, and then click on the **Save as New** button:

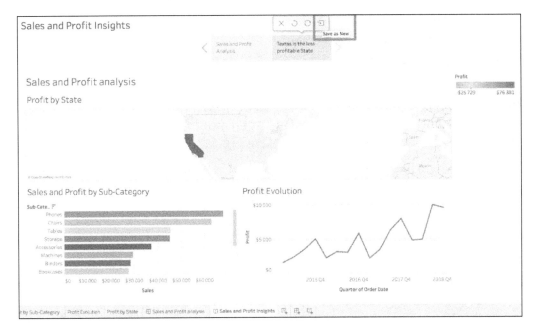

6. The **Save as New** button takes the current state of the Story point and copies it into a new Story point, while reverting the changes of the existing one. You can change the caption of the new Story point to `California is the most profitable State`. Here's the final look of your Story, with three Story points:

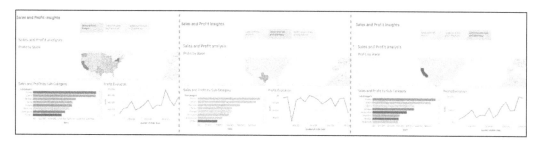

Now that you know how to build a Story, let's see how to customize it.

# Customizing a Story using Story options

There are not many options to customize a Story.

On the left, at the bottom of the **Story** pane, you'll find three options:

- Add **Floating** Text to add some context.
- Show or hide the title of the Story.
- Change the size of the Story.

On the Layout pane, you can change the style of the Story navigator. There are four different styles: **Caption boxes**, **Numbers**, **Dots**, or **Arrows** only. On the same pane, you can also show or hide the arrows. Finally, on the Story top menu, you'll find similar options as for Dashboard: **Format**, **Copy Image**, **Export Image**, and **Clear**.

Stories should not be a mystery to you anymore. Use them to amaze your audience with great insights from your data!

# Summary

Congratulations! This chapter was one of the longest, while also being one of the most important. Building Dashboards is an essential feature of Tableau.

We started with the basics of how to build a Dashboard and the different panes in the workplace, and we also saw the objects that you can add to personalize it. Then, we explored the different types of Layout with all the pros and cons of Tiled and Floating layouts, and Containers. To finish with the Dashboard part, we focused on Actions, how to use them, and how they can add interactivity. After that, we learned about Stories. You learned how, and when, to build and customize them.

In the next chapter, we'll discover a new Tableau product—Tableau Server. All the things you learned from the beginning of the book were about creation—how to create data sources, how to create Worksheets, and how to create Dashboards and Stories.

The next chapter is about sharing; we'll look at how to publish your work to make it globally accessible. Ready to go online?

# 8

# Publishing and Interacting in Tableau Server

It's time to share your work! This chapter is the culmination of everything you've learned since the beginning of the book. It's also the first chapter where you'll use a tool other than Tableau Desktop: Tableau Server/Online.

> As Tableau Server and Tableau Online are almost the same product (you can learn more about this in *Chapter 2, The Tableau Core*), we will use the name Tableau Server for both products throughout this book.

Thanks to Tableau Server, users can connect to new or published data sources to create new analyses and open published Workbooks to interact with them. In this chapter, our main focuses are as follows:

- An introduction to Tableau Server
- Publishing and modifying content
- Interacting with published content

> This book doesn't cover Tableau Server's installation and configuration. This is a technical aspect that requires you to work with your IT team. You can find all the useful information and guidance for installation on the Tableau website: `https://onlinehelp.tableau.com/current/guides/everybody-install/en-us/everybody_admin_intro.htm`.

To reproduce the example in this chapter, you will need access to Tableau Server. Additionally, we are going to use a Tableau Workbook example: World Indicators. You can find it on the start page when you open Tableau, as highlighted in the following screenshot:

# An introduction to Tableau Server

Let's start with the basics. In this section, we will explore what Tableau Server is and look at its contents.

# Basics

Tableau Server is an online tool made for sharing workbooks and data source. Usually, only a few people use Tableau Desktop to build data source and workbooks, which they then publish on Tableau Server, making them available to many users using Tableau Server on the web.

 For Tableau 2019.2, Tableau has changed the design and browsing experience of Tableau Server. We'll focus on this new version in this chapter.

There are two ways of using Tableau Server, as follows:

- In a browser: To access the Tableau Server web page and interact with published content (such as data source, workbooks, and views)
- In Tableau Desktop: To publish data source and workbooks, or connect to published data source and open published workbooks

To connect to Tableau Server on a browser, you have to write the URL of your server and enter your login details and password. If you're using Tableau Online, the URL is https://sso.online.tableau.com.

Tableau Server can have multiple sites; each site is a different environment with different users, groups, and content.

Once you're logged in, you can access the **Home** page of Tableau Server, as shown in the following screenshot:

At the top of the page, you have a search bar to find contents, help and notification icons, and the icon to access your profile. In the left-hand menu, you'll always find the following:

- **Home**: It is the first page and it contains information on the most recent dashboards and what the other users are viewing. You can also use the **Create** button to create a new Project or workbook.

- **Explore**: Here, you can search for the different types of content available in Tableau Server. On the left, you have options to sort, filter, and change the display between a grid and a list.

- **Favorites**: You can click on the star icon of the published content to add it to the favorites page.

- **Recents**: This displays the latest opened content.

With administrator rights, you'll have additional buttons for **Users**, **Groups**, and other settings dedicated to the server administration.

To connect to Tableau Server from Tableau Desktop, go to the **Server** top menu at the top of the page and select **Sign In....** A new window opens, where you can enter your credentials. Once logged in, you can connect to published data source, open-published workbooks, and publish new content on Tableau Server directly from Tableau Desktop. Here's the menu:

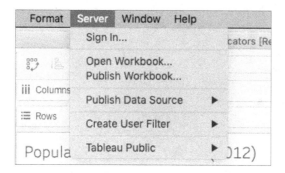

Let's explore the different content you can find on Tableau Server.

# Tableau Server content

There are four different types of content on Tableau Server:

- **Projects**: This is like a folder; you can only create new projects on the web. A project can contain every type of content, and even other projects. The top-level projects are those in the root of Tableau Server.

- **Workbooks**: These are either created directly on Tableau Server or they are published from Tableau Desktop. Each workbook is composed of one or multiple views.

- **Views**: This refers to all the visible Worksheets, dashboards, and stories in the workbooks.

- **Data sources**: This is created on Tableau Desktop and is published here. You can use data source to build new analyses directly on the web or from Tableau Desktop. You can also open Ask Data to use natural language to query your data source.

- **Flows**: This is created with Tableau Prep; you can publish the flow to run them from the web. Thank to the Tableau Prep Conductor add-on. You can learn more about Tableau Prep and Flows here: `https://www.tableau.com/products/prep`

As you can see in the following screenshot, in the **World Indicators Tutorial** project, there is one other subproject, one workbook, and one data source, which are all displayed in the same place:

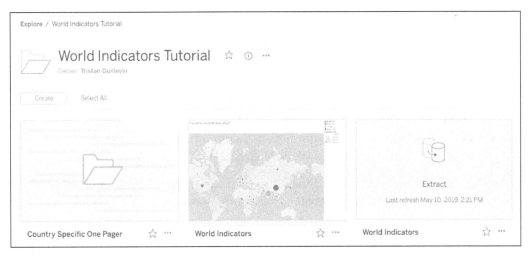

The Sales project dashboard

Let's take a look at how to publish Data Source and Workbooks from Tableau Desktop.

# Publishing and modifying the content

On Tableau Desktop, you can connect to Tableau Server with from the **Sign In...** option in the **Server** top menu. When signed in, you are able to publish data source and workbooks.

Before we start this section, first, create a new project on Tableau Server and name it World Indicators Tutorial – we'll publish our work here.

## Why and how to publish a data source

Tableau Desktop is the only tool that allows you to connect to a dataset, create an extract, publish it to Tableau Server, and schedule an automatic refresh. Publishing a data source offers multiple advantages:

- All the customization (such as aliases, default properties, hidden or renamed fields, and more) is saved. If you or another Tableau Server user uses a published data source, all the customization work is already done.

- All the newly created fields (such as the calculated field, sets, groups, parameters, bins, and more) are also saved. All workbooks that are based on the same published data source use the same calculation. If, for any reason, a calculation needs to change, all the workbooks are impacted at the same time.

- On Tableau Server, you can plan to refresh published data source automatically. All the workbooks that are connected to the same published data source are updated at the same time. You are alerted if a refresh fails.

- On Tableau Server, when you click on a published data source, you can use Ask Data to query the data source by using natural language. With Ask Data, every user is able to find insights and create visualizations.

- Tableau Server users who don't have Tableau Desktop can create new analyses on the web, based on published data source.

If this list doesn't convince you, I don't know what could! If you plan to work in a professional environment with Tableau, publishing a data source is crucial.

 For Tableau Online users, you have to use Tableau Bridge to connect on-premises data to Tableau Online. Learn more about Tableau Bridge here: `https://www.tableau.com/en-gb/products/tableau-bridge`

Publishing a data source is easy: in the **Data** pane (in the Worksheet workplace), right-click on the data source name and click on the **Publish to Server** option. You can also find this option from the **Data** menu in the top of the page. When you click on this option, a new window opens to configure the published data source. In this window, you can do the following:

- Select the project and the name of the data source.

- Add a description and a tag to help understand and find the data source (this is optional).

- Schedule a task to refresh the Extract (optional and only works if the Data Source is an Extract).

- Modify the permissions (you will learn more about this in *Chapter 13, Dealing with Security*).

- Update the workbook to use the published data source (I strongly advise you to use this option).

Using a published data source in a workbook makes it lighter (this is because the extract is no longer inside the workbook but on the server), more secure (you can control a user's access), and sustainable (the changes and updates in the data source are automatically passed on to the workbook).

As an exercise, open the `World Indicators` sample workbook, and publish the Word Indicators data source in the `World Indicators Tutorial` project. Here's the configuration window:

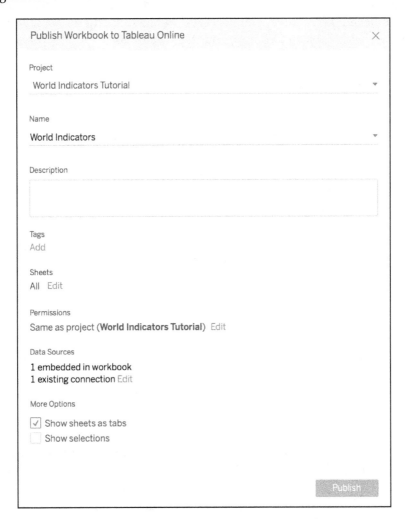

 As you can see, you can't publish a Live data source connected to a file; Tableau automatically generates an extract before publishing it.

Only you and the users of your choice can modify a published data source, making it secure and preventing anyone from making unwanted changes. Unfortunately, this security makes it a bit more complicated to modify a data source; let's discover how to do it next.

# Modifying a published data source

A published data source cannot be modified. You cannot modify the aliases, the groups, the original calculated fields, or any of the other custom fields. In order to modify a published data source, you need to download it, edit the local copy on your computer with Tableau Desktop, and then republish it. Don't worry; it's easier than it sounds!

Instead of **Publish to Server**, a published data source has an equivalent option **Create Local Copy**:

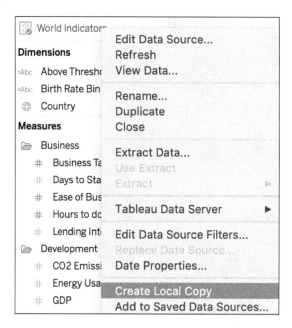

This option automatically downloads the data source and adds it to the workbook as a new data source. When you create a local copy, it appears directly in the **Data** pane:

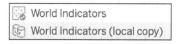

You can make all the modifications you want on the local copy. Then, when you are done, publish your modified data source with the same name as the one you want to replace. To be sure to replace the existing data source, check the message in the published window:

# Publishing a workbook

Publishing a workbook is the best way to share your insights. You can control who has access to your visualizations, and Tableau Server users have many ways of interacting with it. Again, publishing a workbook is straightforward; in the **Server** top menu, you have the **Publish Workbook...** option, as follows:

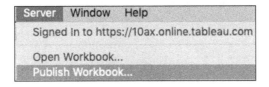

You can publish a workbook without publishing the data source. In that case, the data source is embedded inside the workbook. You can also plan a refresh for workbooks using embedded Data Source (with the condition that you integrate the credentials).

When publishing a workbook, a configuration window opens. In this window, you'll find similar options to publishing a data source (that is, you can choose the project, change the name, add a description and tags, set the permissions, and schedule a refresh extract). However, there are a few new options, as follows:

- Select the visible sheets: The sheets that you decide not to publish are hidden in Tableau Server, but they are still available if you open the workbook in Tableau Desktop.

- Decide whether you want to embed the data source inside the workbook or publish it separately and automatically.

- Show the different sheets as tabs or not (this is usually yes, as you'll want to show the different tabs for the different dashboards in your workbook).

- Show the selections or not (this is usually no unless you want to highlight specific information every time a user opens the workbook).

- Include external files or not (this is usually yes to include shapes and pictures).

Again, as an exercise and for the rest of this chapter, you can publish the **World Indicators** Workbook in the **World Indicators Tutorial** Project:

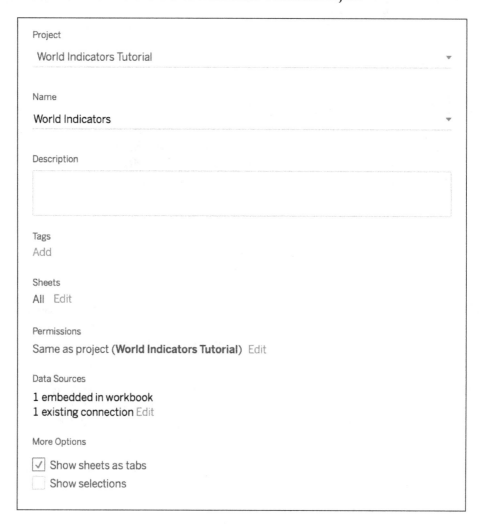

To sum up, publishing your work on Tableau Server is essential when working in an organization. Publishing your Workbook makes your findings and insights available to other users. Sharing your Data Source makes new analysis easier and allows other users to create their own Dashboards without having to rebuild the wheel each time. It also adds security and control over the different fields and harmonizes the definition of the calculations.

In the next section, you'll discover all the different ways of interacting with published content.

# Interacting with published content

Publishing your workbooks and data source presents many more advantages than just sharing them. Tableau Server has many awesome functionalities that are only available online.

If you published the World Indicators data source and workbook in the World Indicators Tutorial project, you should see something similar to the following screenshot in your server:

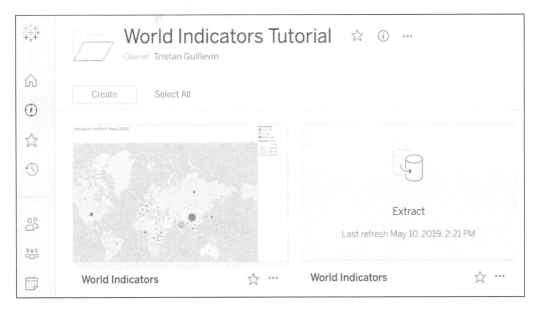

Let's start by discovering all the options you have when you interact with a data source. First, click on the **World Indicators** data source!

# Interacting with published data sources

When you click on a data source on Tableau Server, you open a new page with four different tabs. Three of them are quite simple:

- **Connections**: Here, you can see the different connections of your data source with the ability to edit the information if it is connected to a server.

- **Extract Refreshes**: Here, you'll find here the scheduled refreshes planned for your data source, with the ability to create a new refresh.

- **Connected Workbooks**: Here, you'll find a list of all the workbooks that are connected to this data source.

The first tab is, undoubtedly, the biggest revolution and most important new feature of Tableau Server 2019.1: **Ask Data**. Ask Data allows you to use natural language to query a data source and create a visualization by just asking Tableau, in English, what you want to see.

# Ask Data

Ask Data is the first view that opens when you click on a Data Source. This tool allows you to query any Data Source using the English language.

When Ask Data first opens, Tableau Server starts to analyze the data source to enrich some fields. On the left-hand side, you'll find something similar to the Data pane in Tableau Desktop, and in the middle, a simple search bar with some suggestions:

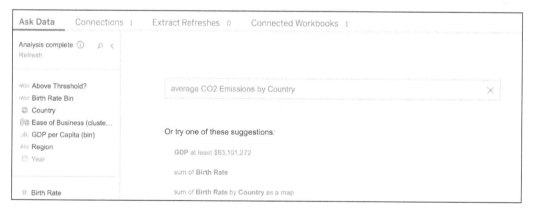

To be honest, the suggestions in the preceding example are quite bad, so let's try something on our own! In the search bar, type in average CO2 Emissions by Country. Ask Data opens a new dedicated tab in your browser and, more importantly, displays something similar to the following screenshot:

Without any knowledge on how to use Tableau to create a visualization, Ask Data was able to convert some text into a visualization. I don't know about you, but I'm very excited about that!

This workplace is quite similar to the good old Worksheet workplace with the Data pane on the left-hand side and the different sheets at the bottom.

> From Tableau Server 2019.2 you can create multiple Worksheets in the Ask Data window!

Speaking of the Data pane on the left-hand side, when you hover over a field, a nice tooltip gives you some quick insights about the number of values, their distribution, and even the calculation if it's a calculated field. But wait, there is more! If you click on the small arrow next to a field, you can use the **Edit synonyms** option. When you add a synonym to a field, you are able to use that synonym in your sentence to create the visualization.

At the top of the page, you can see that the search bar has expanded and suggests that you can adjust the question or use the **Clear All** button to start over. Let's try to add more insights to this map by typing `average GPD` into the textbox:

When you press *Enter*, the query updates to **average COE Emissions and average GDP by Country** and the map changes to circles with the GDP in color and the $CO_2$ emissions in size. The map is not very readable, so why not continue by adding `as scatter plot` to the textbox. When you press *Enter*, the map automatically transforms to a bar chart.

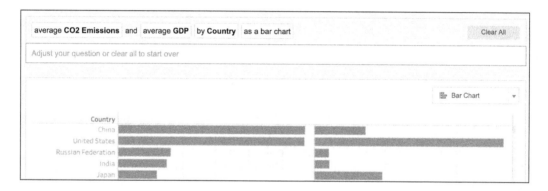

 You could also use the selector on the right-hand side of the visualization to change the Mark type.

If you are satisfied with the visualization but you want to quickly change a Measure or a Dimension, you can click on the different fields in the query box to open a menu allowing you to choose a different field and its aggregation. For example, if you click on **by Country**, you can quickly change it to display the Region instead, as demonstrated in the following screenshot:

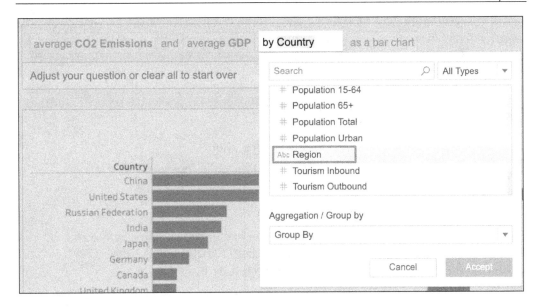

Of course, Ask Data doesn't have the flexibility of Tableau Desktop and you don't have much control over what the result will be. However, it can easily replace a famous demand from the users, *Can you just build a big table where I can search what I want?*. With Ask Data, you don't need that anymore.

When you're done, if you want to save your work, then you can use the **Save** button in the toolbar or close the tab if you don't. Now, let's explore how to interact with your workbooks!

# Interacting with published workbooks

When you click on a workbook in Tableau Server, you can see all its views (that is, Worksheets, dashboards, and stories). Then, when you click on a view, Tableau Server opens it in reader mode. You cannot modify it, but you can use the filters, highlighters, parameters, actions, and see the tooltips.

On top, there is the navigation bar with the current path to the view and some icons allowing you to open the device layout preview, see the data sources, and the other default options (such as search, favorites, help, and notifications):

Below the navigation bar, there is a special toolbar with some Tableau Server-specific features. The left part (which is not very interesting even if it is useful) allows you to **Undo, Redo,** or **Revert** all your actions, and **Refresh** or **Pause** the data source. You won't use that part much.

Additionally, there are Height features available only on Tableau Server, including the following:

- **Edit** is explained in the *Web Authoring* section
- **Share** provides a link to the View and the code for embedding it in a web page
- **Full Screen** speaks for itself

We'll focus more on the five other features. For each feature, you can test and reproduce the examples using the **Tourism** View of the `World Indicators` workbook published earlier, which is highlighted here:

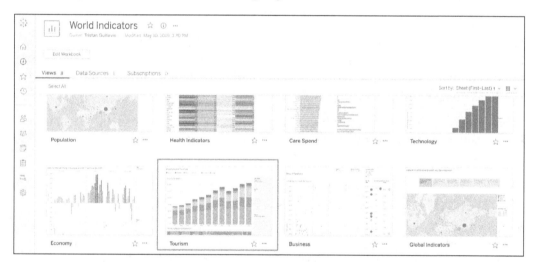

The Tourism View of the World Indicators workbook

Let's start with **Custom Views**.

# Custom views

A custom view is a way of saving the current state of a visualization to reopen it later. Imagine that, in a dashboard, you need to select different values in many different filters to focus the visualization on what really interests you. Without custom views, you'll have to apply the different filters each time you open the workbook.

With custom views, you can save the state where all the filters are applied, and reopen the dashboard on that state whenever you want, with all the filters applied at once.

[  The default view is **Original**. It's the view as the author of the workbook published it. ]

To add a custom view, click on the **View: Original** button to open the configuration window. This window offers different interesting options, including the following:

- **Make it my default**: Each time you open the workbook, it will be this custom view that will open by default.
- **Make it public**: The other Tableau Server users are able to see and use your custom view.
- **My Views**: The list of all the custom views that you created for this view.
- **Other Views**: The list of all the other public custom views created by other users.
- **Manage**: With the **Manage** button, you can rename, delete, or hide your custom views.

Let's take a look at a quick example on the Tourism View together:

1. Use the quick filters to start the **Year Range** filter in 2005 and select Europe in the region.
2. Click on **View: Original**.

3. In the configuration window, name your custom view Europe, starting in 2005, make it your default, and then click on **Save**. The configuration window should look like the following screenshot:

4. Click on **World Indicators** in the very top of the window to go back to the list of views:

5. Reopen the **Tourism** view; you should be automatically filtered in Europe, after 2005.

6. Click on the **View: Europe, starting in 2005** toolbar button and uncheck the **Make it my default** option to reuse the original view as your default one.

This option is a time saver when you have to apply many different filters, or if a team only focuses on a subset of the data. The second feature is probably just as important and useful!

# Alert

With alerts, Tableau sends you an email when a condition is fulfilled in your View after a refresh. For example, if you have a visualization with daily sales, you can configure an alert to receive an email when the sales are above or below a certain amount. An alert is a great way to allow you to do something other than checking your dashboard every day on Tableau Server. You can set an alert on any visualization as long as it has an axis.

 Make sure that the SMTP server is configured and that you have specified a correct email address.

To create an alert, click on the **Alert** button in the toolbar. Since Tableau 2019.2, a new, **Alerts**, opens on the right-side. To add an alert, select an axis and then click on the **Create** button. Once you've done that, Tableau Server opens a configuration window, where you can configure the following:

- The **Condition** and the **Threshold** to trigger the alert. Tableau indicates to you whether the condition is currently true or not.

- The **Subject** of the email and the frequency at which it is sent.

- The **Recipients** of the email (you can specify multiple users who will receive the email).

- The visibility of the alert to allow other users to view and use it.

In the right-hand pane, you'll find all the visible alerts that exist for the current View. You have the ability to subscribe to an existing alert with the **Add me** button. If you created the alert, you'll be able to edit, delete, or change the owner of this alert by using the **Actions** menu:

Let's create an alert for the Tourism View:

1. Click on the **Alert** button to open the **Alerts** pane.
2. Click on the axis of the `Income by Region` visualization (it turns blue when selected), and then click on the **Create** button in the **Alerts** pane.

3. Configure the alert to send you an email with the subject, `Tourism Income above 1,250B!`, when the value is **Above or equal to** `1,250,000,000,000`. If you didn't filter a specific region, then the condition is true for the year 2012. The configuration window should look like the following screenshot:

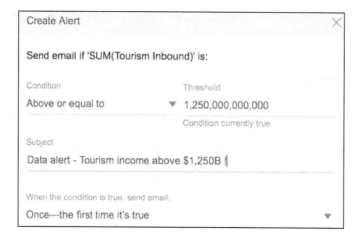

4. Click on the **Create Alert** button. You should see the alert appear in the **Alerts** pane.

5. Refresh the page and click on the **Alert** button in the toolbar. You should see that the alert was triggered a few seconds earlier.

6. If your email address is correct, then you should have received an email with a screenshot of the dashboard and the alert.

As you can see, the alert feature is very useful, and probably just as much as the next one: subscribe!

# Subscribe

If you subscribe to a view or workbook, you'll receive, at a chosen frequency, an email with snapshots of your visualizations. Like alerts, it's a useful feature that allows you to receive insights directly into your inbox, without having to connect to Tableau Server. Each snapshot contains a link to the published visualizations, so if you spot something intriguing, click on the picture to automatically open the View in Tableau Server and start your analysis.

To subscribe, click on the **Subscribe** button in the toolbar and configure it on the window that opens. Here's a screenshot of the **Subscribe** configuration window:

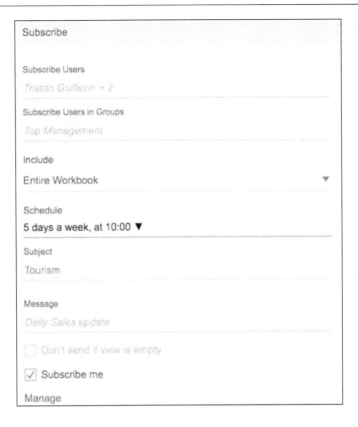

There are many interesting options in this window, including the following:

- Define the **Users** and **Groups** who will receive the emails.
- Specify whether the subscription is only for **This View** or the **Entire Workbook** (there will be a snapshot of every view in the workbook in the email).
- Specify the **Schedule** and repetition of the emails.
- Modify the **Subject** of the email and add a **Message**.
- **Manage** the subscriptions and add or remove users.

The next useful feature to discover is download.

# Download

When you click on the **Download** button, a new window opens with six options. Four of these options are available by default:

- **Image**: This generates a picture of the view.
- **PDF**: This generates a PDF of the current View or the entire workbook. You can specify the scaling and format of the PDF.
- **PowerPoint**: This generates a PPTX file with each view of the workbook in a specific slide.
- **Workbooks**: This downloads the file.

To activate the two other options, you need to click on a visualization. If you click on a mark, you will download the data of that mark. Unfortunately, there is no way to see which Worksheet is selected. The two options are as follows:

- **Data**: This opens the summary data, but you can also get the full data on the second tab.
- **Crosstab**: This generates a CSV file that you can download.

The final feature, unlike the previous ones, isn't about interacting with the View, but with other users.

# Comments

When you click on the **Comments** button, a Right-hand pane opens where you can chat with other users. Each workbook's views have their proper comments. Any user (who is allowed to do so) can add a comment, mention other users, and add a snapshot of the current view.

Comments are a great way for you to add more information about your views. Other users can also use this feature if they spot mistakes or if they have questions.

As you will now understand, publishing a workbook isn't just about making it safe and visible for other users. Some features, such as alerts or subscribe, open completely new ways of working with your data. To finish the section, let's end with how to preview the device layouts directly from Tableau Server.

# The mobile layout preview

Since Tableau 2019.1, you can preview the different layouts on Tableau Server. Above the toolbar, a new button, **Preview Device Layouts**, is now available, as highlighted in the following screenshot:

When you click on the button, Tableau opens the preview mode where you can select **Laptop**, **Tablet**, or **Phone** to see how your dashboard renders on those different devices.

This new feature is a great addition to test your different layouts without having to use those devices or special tools.

Let's take a look at the last way of interacting with Tableau Server contents with Web Authoring.

# Web Authoring

Web Authoring is the ability to add new data sources and build new workbooks directly from Tableau Server on the web. There are three main ways of opening Web Authoring mode.

> The interface is almost identical to Tableau Desktop, with the Data pane on the left-hand side. You can create new Worksheets, new dashboards, and stories as if you were in Tableau Desktop.

This first way to open Web Authoring mode is by clicking on the **Edit** button when interacting with a view. If you click on this button, Tableau opens the Web Authoring mode where you can modify your workbook without leaving Tableau Server – it's a great way to fix small issues.

The second way to open Web Authoring mode is by starting a new workbook from a published data source. When you open a data source on Tableau Server, just below its name, there is a button, **New Workbook**, which you can use to create new content:

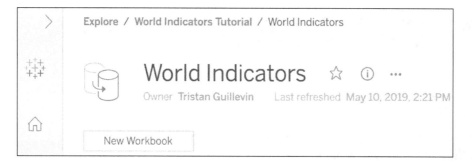

The final way to open Web Authoring mode is to click on the **Create** button from the Home or Explore page and select **Workbook**. Then, Tableau opens Web Authoring mode and starts by asking you to connect to the data. With a creator license, you can connect to files and servers directly from the web! There are four types of data connections available, as follows:

- **File**: Drag and drop an Excel file or CSV file on the web page; you can choose the **Sheets** option and build a new data source.

- **Connectors**: A list of server-hosted databases available directly from Tableau Server.

- **On this site**: Use an existing published data source.

- **Dashboard starters**: Start with prebuilt templates of cloud-based systems.

Again, you won't be lost; all the different Workspaces are similar to Tableau Desktop.

 Users who don't have a creator license can always use published data sources to create new analyses, but they can't connect to new data from files or servers.

Not all the functionalities of Tableau Desktop are available yet on the web editor, but it's getting closer and closer after each new version of Tableau Server. It is, however, an excellent way of allowing new users to create their analyses and train future Tableau Desktop users.

# Summary

Now that you've learned how to use Tableau Server, you have a complete view of what Tableau can do as a data visualization and analysis tool. We looked at connecting data to Tableau Desktop, building your data source, Worksheets and dashboards, and finally publishing all your work online for you and other users to interact with. What a journey!

This chapter was the last piece of the puzzle in understanding how to use Tableau. You started by understanding what Tableau Server is and what kind of content you can find in it. Then, you learned how to publish your content, modify it, and interact with it on the web.

This summary may sound like the end – what else could be left to see now? A lot! In the next chapters, we'll get our hands back on Tableau Desktop to discover many other crucial and advanced features. Creating parameters, using the analytics built-in tools, using data blending, securing your data, and many more features are waiting to be discovered. Without any more teasing, let's start with calculated fields, and how to unlock unlimited power on Tableau Desktop.

# Section 3: Advanced features

In this section, we will create some calculated fields in Tableau. This section will cover the basis of calculations in Tableau and will alert you to some easy-to-make mistakes. We will also cover analysis tools and explain them in depth. We will then browse through the security requirements in Tableau. We'll demonstrate how to secure projects and their elements (such as the workbook and data source). Finally, we'll go through their different roles and all the options with clear explanations.

This section will include the following chapters:

- *Chapter 9, An Introduction to Calculations*
- *Chapter 10, Analytics and Parameters*
- *Chapter 11, Advanced Data Connections*
- *Chapter 12, Dealing with Security*

# An Introduction to Calculations

Congratulations! You have reached the first advanced chapter of this book! This is a challenging chapter, yet essential if you want to use Tableau without limitations. Indeed, to build the best analysis, you'll need to create calculations. But let me reassure you: if you are traumatized by words such as *universe*, *cube*, or *MDX*, you can breathe. Creating a calculation in Tableau is straightforward, and the language is very close to what you find in Excel. This chapter is split into two main sections:

- Calculated field basics
- Advanced functions

In this chapter, some examples use the `Sample-Superstore` saved data source, but others require special files. You can find the files that are used for the tutorials on my website, `https://tableau2019.ladataviz.com`, in *Chapter 9*, *An Introduction to Calculations*.

## Calculated field basics

A Calculated Field is a new field in your data source. It can have any data type and be a Measure or Dimension. To differentiate a field from a calculated field, each data type icon has a small equals (=) symbol in front of it, as you can see in the following screenshot:

| | |
|---|---|
| =# | Profit Ratio |
| # | Quantity |

Let's start by learning how to create a Calculated Field.

# Creating a Calculated Field

To create a new Calculated Field, go through the following steps:

1.  Click on the small arrow next to **Dimensions** in the **Data** pane, which is highlighted in the following screenshot, and select Create Calculated Field:

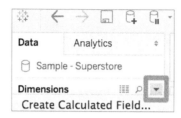

2.  It's also possible to right-click on a field and go to **Create** to start a new Calculated Field based on this field. You can edit a Calculated Field when you right-click on it.

3.  When you create a new Calculated Field, a new window opens in which you have to write a formula. The formula can be based on other fields and use functions.

4.  On the right, when you click on the arrow, you can open the list of functions.

5.  When you write a formula, at the bottom of the window, Tableau indicates to you whether the calculation is valid or not. You can also see the dependencies (other Calculated Fields and Sheets that use this Calculated Field).

6.  Click on **OK** when you are done, and the calculation will be valid.

Here's an example of the calculation window with the list of functions:

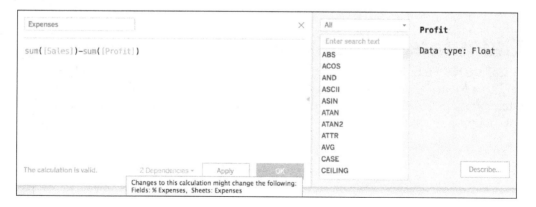

When you write a formula, the fields will be in orange and between brackets and the functions will be in blue.

Formulas handle auto-completion, meaning that when you start writing autocompletion, meaning that when you start writing at least one character, Tableau opens a list of suggestions based on all the fields and functions available. You just have to press *Enter* or click on the desired element.

You can also drag and drop any field in the calculation window to add it to the formula.

When using existing fields in a formula, you can decide whether to aggregate them or not; let's discover what the difference is.

# To aggregate or not to aggregate fields

The main rule when you create a calculated measure is to think about the aggregation. As you already know, a Measure is, by default, aggregated, and so are calculated measures. You can specify the aggregation inside the formula or not:

- If you aggregate the data inside the formula, the pill of the calculated Measure will start with AGG

- If you don't specify the aggregation in the formula, a default one will be added when you use the field in the View, as it would for any normal measure

For example, the **Profit Ratio** field in the Sample - Superstore saved data source contains the aggregations inside the formula SUM([Profit])/SUM([Sales]) formula. If you use this field in the View, the pill will start with AGG.

A Calculated Field cannot contain aggregated and nonaggregated fields in the same formula. Remember that you can aggregate a Dimension with the ATTR() function.

Often, there will be a significant difference between adding the aggregation inside the formula and not adding it. For the calculation of the **Profit Ratio**, Tableau first aggregates the Profit and the Sales separately, then divides the two aggregated results. An incorrect way of calculating the **Profit Ratio** would be [Profit]/ [Sales]. With this calculation, Tableau divides the value of the **Profit** by the **Sales** at each line of the data source, then aggregates the result of all the divisions. To illustrate this, I created a Calculated Field, Wrong Profit Ratio, with the incorrect formula. Here's the difference between the two calculations:

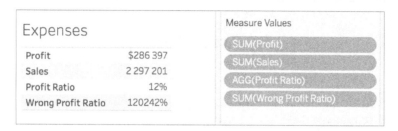

As you can see, if Tableau sums the result of all the divisions rather than dividing two aggregated values, the result is incorrect. Always keep this principle in mind.

# Using calculation functions

Of course, you can create Calculated Fields based on a calculation between different fields (such as the Profit Ratio); however, the really interesting aspect of Calculated Fields is the functions. There are many different functions; some basic, some hard to understand. Each function returns a specific data type, and some require arguments.

Tableau has made this easy: each function has a clear description and examples for learning how to use them.

Going through all the functions and repeating the description and example that's already available in Tableau doesn't add any value. My strong advice for you is to take fifteen minutes to look at all the functions to have a clear overview of what you can and can't do.

Here's an example of the round function:

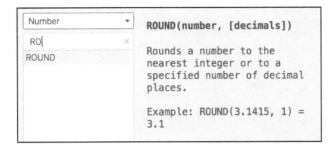

In the following sections and chapters, we'll often use calculations, so don't be afraid—you'll practice them. Speaking of practice, it's time for a guided tutorial!

# Example – highlighting values

Probably the most common use of a calculation is to highlight values. Let's create a calculation that returns different text values depending on sales:

1.  Open Tableau Desktop and click on the **Sample – Superstore** saved data source.

2.  Create a new Calculated Field and name it `Sales Highlight`.

3.  Write the following formula and check that the calculation is valid: `if SUM([Sales]) > 300000 then "Great" ELSEIF SUM([Sales]) < 50000 then "Bad" else "Average" END`.

> This formula is a conditional test. If the sum of the sales is higher than 300,000, the formula returns `Great`; if the sum of the sales is lower than 50,000, the formula returns `Bad`; otherwise, the formula returns `Average`.

4.  Create a visualization with **Sales** in **Columns**, **Sub-Category** in **Rows**, and **Sales Highlight** in **Color**.

5. You can change the color of the three values to make it easier to see the difference between **Great** and **Bad** values. Here's the final result:

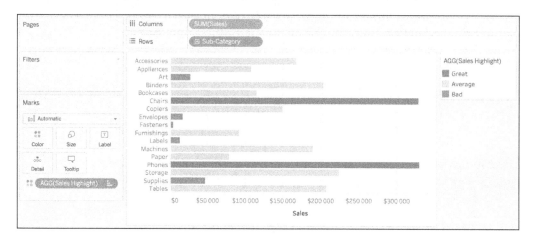

As you can see, simple calculations can already be useful. In the next section, we'll see how we can use two sorts of advanced functions: Table Calculation and Level of Detail.

# Advanced functions

There are two types of functions that are a bit different: Table Calculation and Level of Detail.

# Table Calculation

The Table Calculation functions are special in many ways. Mastering them requires practice, but they are very useful. It's important to understand how they work and how to use them. Let's start slowly by using an awesome option called **Quick Table Calculation**.

# Quick Table Calculation

**Quick Table Calculation** is an option that becomes available with a right-click on every Measure. It automatically changes the Measure to a Calculated Measure using a Table Calculation function.

You can find very interesting functions among the Quick Table Calculations list: Running Sum, Rank, Difference, Percentage of Total, and many more—all available with a single right-click.

As an example, let's compare, for each year, the cumulative sales by quarter using the `Sample - Superstore` data source:

1. On a blank Worksheet, add **Order Date** to **Columns** and **Sales** to **Rows**.

2. Click on the **+** button next to the **YEAR(Order Date)** pill to add **QUARTER**. The visualization should look as follows:

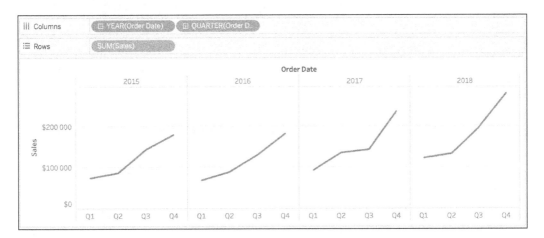

3. Right-click on **Sales**, go to **Quick-Table Calculation**, and select **Running Total**. What you will see is the running total of the **Sales** across all years and quarters.

4. Put the **YEAR(Order Date)** pill in **Color**. It's now very easy to see which year ends with the most Sales generated at the end of the year; you can see this in the following screenshot:

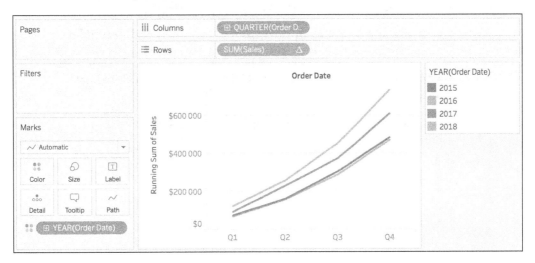

Quick Table Calculations are great and simple to use. Sometimes, you may want to create more advanced calculations using Table Calculation functions.

## Table Calculation functions

Table Calculation functions, such as **WINDOW, LOOKUP,** or **INDEX,** allow you to create advanced Calculated Fields. You can quickly spot a <u>Calculated Field</u> that uses a Table Calculation function by the triangle icon in its pill: .

A standard calculated Measure is computed for every row in the Data Source, and then aggregated when used in the View. When using a Table function, it's a bit different:

- The calculation is computed after the aggregation and is based on the displayed result in the View. Modifying the View (the sort, for example) directly affects the Table Calculation.

- When you right-click on a Table Calculation pill, you will find two new options:

  ° **Compute using**: This allows you choose how to compute the calculation and the ability

  ° **Edit Table Calculation...**: This opens a new window where you can use the calculation assistance to help you see how the calculation will be computed

It's normal to still be a bit confused, but let's remedy that by creating an example together.

## Hands-on – Table Calculation functions

Let's create a visualization with the table functions computed at different levels using the `Sample - Superstore` saved data source. Let's start simply:

1. On a blank worksheet, put **Region** in **Columns**, and then **Category** and **Sales** in **Columns**.

2. In the toolbar, click on the icon to display the label—that is, . Here's the result:

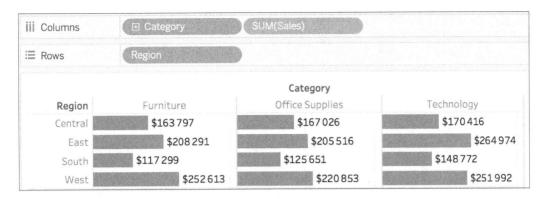

Our goal is to highlight the highest sales value. Since we have two dimensions in the view, there are two options: either show the maximum value for each Region or for each Category. You can easily achieve this with Table Calculation functions. Follow these steps to set this up:

1. Create a new calculated field and name it `Highest Value`.

2. Write the following calculation and check that it is valid: `SUM([Sales]) = WINDOW_MAX(SUM([Sales]))`.

> The `WINDOW_MAX()` function is a function that returns the maximum value in the *window*. The *window* is defined by the **Compute Using** option of the Table calculation. The formula returns `True` if the value of `SUM(Sales)` is the highest value of the *window*, or `False` otherwise.

3. Put the calculation in **Color** (and update the color if you want). By default, the Table Calculation is computed on **Table (down)**, which in our case is the Region, thereby showing the Region with the highest sales for each Category. Here's the result:

4. Maybe you prefer to see which Category is the best for each Region. To do that, right-click on the **Highest Value** pill, go to **Compute using**, and select **Table (across)**. You should see the same result that's shown in the following screenshot:

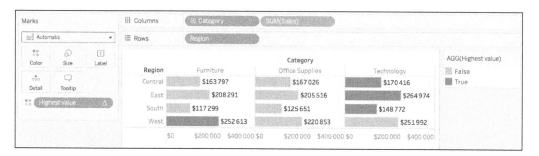

Table Calculation functions aren't easy to understand, and they will require practice to be mastered. It's important that you know they exist, what you can do with them, and how to use them.

The next set of functions are called **Level of Detail (LOD)** functions, and are even more powerful.

# Level of Detail

Level-of-Detail (LOD) functions were introduced in version 9 of Tableau and, today, it's hard to believe that there was a time without them! These functions are probably the most powerful ones. The FIXED function, in particular, allows you to ignore Filters, ignore duplication in your data, and return a Measure that's aggregated on the dimension of your choice. Let's start with the basics of these functions.

## LOD function basics

As you already know, each Dimension in the View splits the number of Marks and defines the level of detail for the aggregation of the Measures. However, at some point, you will probably need to aggregate a Measure at a different level than the one on the View. To do this, you can use one of the three LOD functions—namely, INCLUDE, EXCLUDE, or FIXED:

- **INCLUDE** adds the specified Dimensions to the level of detail of the aggregation—for example, the `{ INCLUDE [Region]: SUM([Sales]) }` calculation aggregates the Sales by Region and all the other Dimensions in the View.

- **EXCLUDE** removes the specified Dimensions from the LOD of the aggregation—for example, the { EXCLUDE [Region]: SUM([Sales])} calculation aggregates the Sales by all the Dimensions in the View except the Region.

- **FIXED** can do both, as you have to specify all the Dimensions of the level of detail precisely—for example, the { FIXED [Region]: SUM([Sales])} calculation aggregates Sales with Region only, no matter the other Dimensions in the View.

 INCLUDE and EXCLUDE calculations are always Measures and as a consequence are aggregated. FIXED can be either a Dimension or a Measure.

You can write all the INCLUDE and EXCLUDE functions with FIXED. Let's focus on the third LOD function, which is the most powerful one.

# FIXED

With FIXED, all the Dimensions that you want to include in the level of detail must be specified, so if you want to exclude an existing Dimension, don't specify it, and if you want to include one, specify it.

Calculated fields that use a FIXED function have three advantages. First, they are easier to understand than INCLUDE or EXCLUDE. You write the Dimensions that you want to use, and that's it—Tableau only uses them to aggregate the calculation, no matter what's in the View.

The second advantage is even more interesting: FIXED calculations are not impacted by Dimension filters. As you may remember, the Filter hierarchy looks like this:

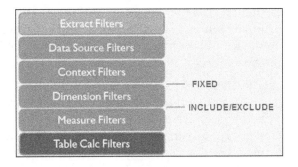

As you can see, the INCLUDE and EXCLUDE functions are impacted by the Dimension filters, but not FIXED unless they are in Context.

Let's see how we can use this to our advantage with an example. Let's display three different Measures by Sub-Category, with a filter on State to keep only California. The three Measures are:

- A normal aggregation, that is, the sum of sales: SUM([Sales])

- A FIXED calculation: SUM( { FIXED [Sub-Category]: SUM([Sales]) } )

- The ratio of the two previous Measures: SUM([Sales]) / SUM( { FIXED [Sub-Category]: SUM([Sales]) } )

Here's the result:

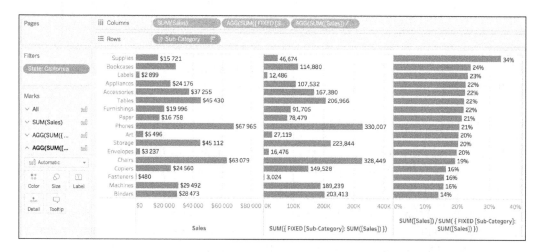

Let's spend some time look at the result in more detail:

- The first value is a simple aggregation. It returns the sum of Sales by **Sub-Category**, filtered on California.

- The second calculation, SUM( { FIXED [Sub-Category]: SUM([Sales]) } ), returns the total sum of Sales by **Sub-Category** for all States. As State is not specified in the list of Dimensions in the FIXED function; the filter has no power over this calculation.

- The third calculation, SUM([Sales]) / SUM( { FIXED [Sub-Category]: SUM([Sales]) } ), calculates the ratio between the two previous calculations. This ratio represents the percentage of Sales made in California for each Sub-Category. You can see that a third of all the Supplies sales are made in California.

It's a typical use case of the useful FIXED calculation.

The third and last advantage is also very useful: FIXED allows you to remove duplicates in your data. Since you can specify the level of detail of a Measure, you can return the unique value of a Measure (with MAX or MIN) by its unique row identifier. Hard to picture? The following hands-on tutorial shows you how to deduplicate your data.

# Hands-on – using an LOD function to deduplicate your data

In the following example, we'll add a Target for each Category. The Target table contains two columns, Category and Target, as you can see in the following screenshot:

| Category | Target |
|----------|--------|
| Technology | 7000 |
| Office Supplies | 20000 |
| Furniture | 10000 |

For this example, download the Superstore with Target Excel file from my blog, https://tableau2019.ladataviz.com, in **Chapter 9: An Introduction to Calculations** section. The direct link is https://ladataviz.com/wp-content/uploads/2018/09/Superstore-with-Target.xls. This Excel file contains two sheets, Orders and Target.

Let's add a target to our orders and deduplicate the data thanks to the FIXED function:

1. Open Tableau and connect to the Superstore with Target Excel file.

2. Create a Join between the two tables on Category. As you can see, the Target value is duplicated:

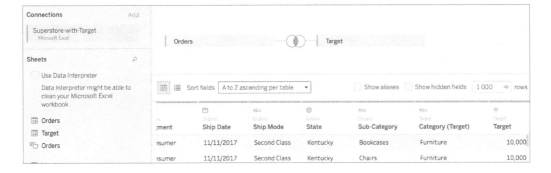

3. In a worksheet, add `Target` in Text. The current sum of Target is 154 659 000. Good luck reaching that!. As you can see, the value is way above the expected sum of targets.

4. Create a Calculated Field, name it `Target - fixed`, and write the calculation `{FIXED [Category]:MIN([Target])}`.

5. Add the new calculation, `Target - fixed`, in the text. You should see *37,000*, which is the expected value of the sum of the targets.

That's it! You can now use the **Target - fixed** calculation in all the Worksheets or other calculations; it'll always be calculated correctly.

As you can see, Fixed is a very useful function for removing duplicates, ignoring Filters, and specifying precisely the LOD of a Measure. Always be sure to put the Filters in Context if you want them to have an impact on the Fixed calculation.

# Summary

This chapter is a door opened to unlimited power. With the right dataset and calculations, you can build absolutely anything you want. Yes, it requires a bit, and sometimes, a lot of practice, but mastering Tableau goes through this. As the title of this book says, we're only getting started here!

In this chapter, you learned the basics of Calculated Fields. With simple examples, you learned why aggregation is so important, created your first calculations, and used your first Tableau functions. In the second part of this chapter, things started to get a bit more complicated, as we looked at two types of special functions: Table Calculation and LOD. Table functions are applied after the aggregations and can be computed in various ways. You can use them to calculate ranks, difference, percentages of totals, and more. LOD can ignore dimension filters and even remove duplication. Both are powerful; both require practice.

In the next chapter, you'll learn how to use all the analytics tools provided by Tableau to add Trend Lines, Clusters, Forecasts, and more. Then, you'll create Parameters to bring more interactivity to your visualizations. Finally, with the help of calculations (*I told you, this chapter is crucial*), you'll create one of the most efficient and useful visualizations by combining Parameters, Analytics tools, and Calculated Fields!

# 10
# Analytics and Parameters

Analytics and parameters are two significant but easy ways to enhance your work. Analytics tools offer new insights, such as **Trend Line**, **Forecast**, and **Cluster**. With **Parameters**, you'll discover a new way of bringing interactivity to your visualizations with user inputs.

In this chapter, we'll cover the following topics:

- Using built-in Analytics tools
- How to work with Parameters
- Creating a year-over-year comparison

If you went through all the chapters prior to this one, you know what data source we'll be using! If this is the first chapter you are reading, all the examples and a guided tutorial can be reproduced with the `Sample - Superstore` data source, which you can find on the first page when opening Tableau.

## Using built-in Analytics tools

When creating a visualization on a Worksheet, you will have always used the **Data** pane on the left; that is, until now! Under the preceding data source name, you can see that there are two tabs: **Data** and **Analytics**. If you click on **Analytics**, Tableau opens a new pane, divided into three parts: **Summarize**, **Model**, and **Custom**.

This is highlighted in the following screenshot:

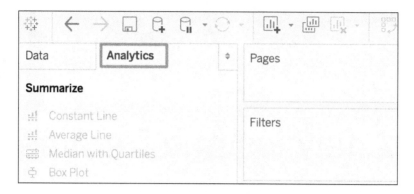

 All the options on the **Analytics** pane can be found in other places in Tableau (with a right-click on an axis or the **Analysis** menu at the top of the page). The options in the **Analytics** pane are mostly just shortcuts or preconfigured options.

Let's explore all the options of each section. All of them can be used with a simple drag and drop.

# The Summarize tab

In the **Summarize** tab, you can find options to add a reference Line, Band, Box Plot, or Totals. Let's look at a quick overview of each option, starting with Constant Line.

## Constant Line

By double-clicking on **Constant Line** or by dragging and dropping into the View, you can automatically add a Constant Line to your visualization. When you add one, Tableau opens a small textbox where you can enter the value of the constant. A Constant Line is an excellent way of representing a goal.

For example, the goal could be to have sales exceeding $450,000 for each Region. As you can see in the following screenshot, it's straightforward to spot the Regions that have exceeded or are yet to achieve the goal with a Constant Line:

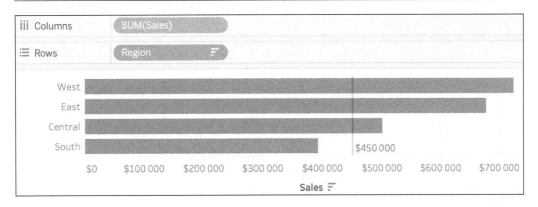

With a simple click on the line, you can change the value of the constant, change its format, or remove it. Let's continue with the second, very similar option: **Average Line**.

# Average Line

Average Line works in the same way as Constant Line; however, you don't enter any values. Instead, Tableau automatically calculates the average of the Measure. When you start to drag **Average Line** into the View, Tableau displays a menu where you can drop the option on **Table**, **Pane**, or **Cell**, as shown in the following screenshot:

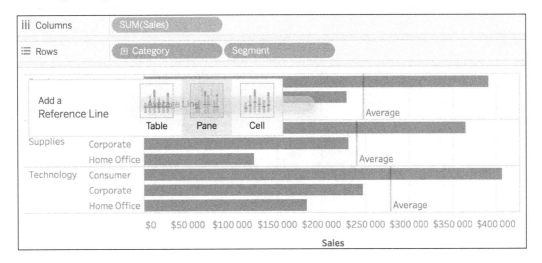

The following descriptions of the icons will help you understand the difference between the three options:

- **Table**: Tableau draws a unique line that is the average of all the **Marks**
- **Pane**: Tableau draws as many lines as there are intersections between the Dimensions (in the preceding example, there are three lines)
- **Cell**: Tableau draws a line for each different value (so it's usually not very useful when using averages)

When you click on Average Line, you can edit the default aggregation average, to make it median or sum, for example. If you click on **Edit**, Tableau opens a menu where you can customize the Average Line. We'll look at what else we can do in this window in the *The Custom tab* section.

The next option combines a reference Line and Distribution Band.

## Median with Quartiles

This option creates a **Median with Quartiles** and a **Distribution Band** with upper and lower quartiles. As for the Average Line, you can create a **Median with Quartiles** on the **Table**, **Pane**, or **Cell**. Here's an example:

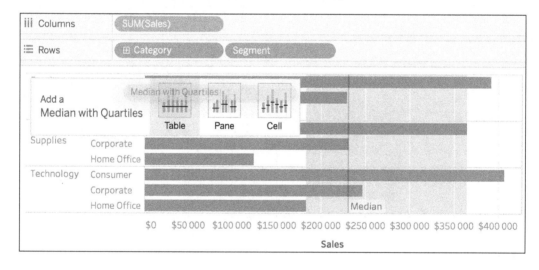

After adding it, if you right-click on the axis and go to **Edit Reference Line**, you can see that you can configure the Median Line and the Quartiles Distribution separately. You can also configure them with a click on the line or on the border of the quartiles.

The next option, Box Plot, only works under certain conditions.

# Box Plot

The **Box Plot** option is only available when there is more than one unstacked Mark per cell. A Box Plot may be hard to read for people who don't come from a statistical background, but it's a great tool for viewing the dispersion in your data and spotting outliers. Here's an example of a Box Plot:

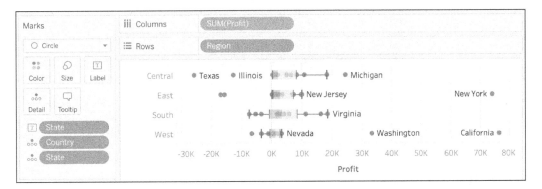

This example shows the profit made by each Region, with one circle per state. As you can see, you can easily spot the outliers as *Texas* and *California*.

The last Summarize option is a classic option called **Totals**.

# Totals

When you start to drag **Totals** into the View, Tableau displays a new menu where you can specify whether you want to add the Subtotals, the Column Grand Totals, or the Row Grand Totals.

Tableau uses the default property, Total using, of the Measure to choose the aggregation. Here's an example of Subtotals and Column Grand Totals:

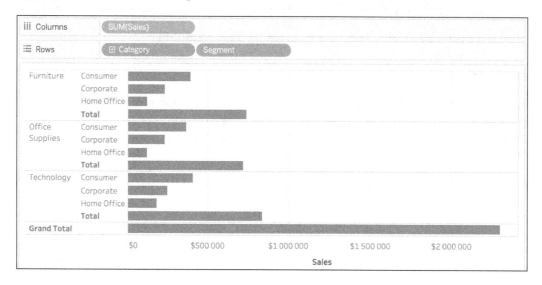

Now, let's explore a new set of options, which are under the **Model** tab.

# The Model tab

The options under **Model** don't just add a new aggregation to summarize your data, but add new statistical models such as Cluster, Trend Line, and Forecast. Using them is as simple as in the previous section; drag and drop them into the View.

## Average or median with a confidence interval

The first two options are similar to Average Line or Median Line. The only difference is the addition of a confidence interval of 95%.

The next option is, this time, very different compared to what you've seen before.

## Trend Line

You can only add a Trend Line when you have two continuous fields on opposing axes (one on Rows and one on Columns). A Trend Line can be used to view a trend of a Measure over time or the correlation between two Measures.

To add a Trend Line, drag and drop the option into the View. By default, the Trend Model that's used is linear. You can specify the Trend Model to use when you drag and drop the option.

 It's also possible to add a Trend Line with a right-click on the View.

Here's an example of the usage of Trend Lines:

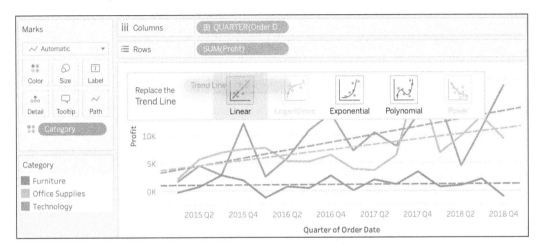

As you can see, it's easy to see that the profits are growing for **Office Supplies** and **Technology**, but are stagnating for **Furniture**.

When you hover over a Trend Line, you can see information about the Trend Model. If you right-click on the Trend Line, you can open an advanced description of the Trend Line and the Trend Model or open the **Edit Trend Lines...** window, where you can change the Trend Model and customize it.

For the next option, a Date is mandatory.

# Forecast

Forecast is a great option when you have Date fields in your data source. You can only add a Forecast when you're displaying a Measure through a continuous date. Tableau calculates the forecast based on the existing data points. To add a **Forecast**, drag and drop the option into the View or select **Show Forecast** from the right-click options.

When you add a forecast, the Measure is replaced by a Forecast Measure, and the **Forecast indicator** is added in **Color**. Here's an example of the forecast of the Profit by **Continuous Quarter** of **Order Date**:

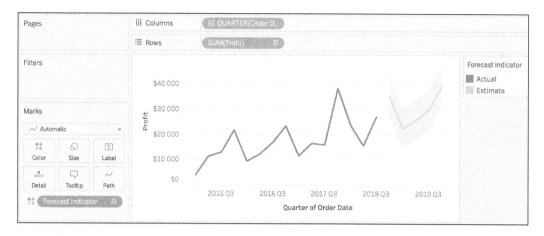

Great news, **Profit** is forecast to grow! When you right-click on the View, if you hover over **Forecast**, you can find a description of the Forecast Model and some options for configuring the Forecast.

Last but not least, is cluster.

# Cluster

To add a cluster, you need to have at least one Measure and one Dimension in the View. To add a cluster, double-click on the option or drag and drop it into the View.

Here's an example of four clusters on the subcategories by **Sales** and **Profit**:

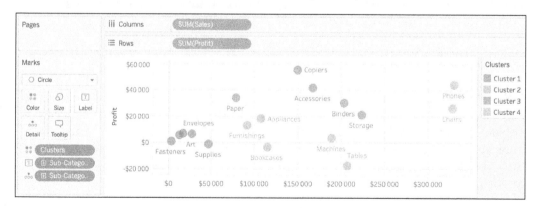

When you add a Cluster, Tableau opens a window where you can add or remove variables (Measure or Dimension) and define the number of Clusters. Then, Tableau adds a new generated pill, **Clusters**, on **Color**. You can use this generated pill wherever you want in the View (for another property or in filters, for example) or drag and drop it among the fields in your data source to add it as a new field. Like the other model options, you can right-click on the **Clusters** pill to edit it or view the model's description.

To finish with this section, let's look at the Custom analytics options. Be careful; this will be fast!

# The Custom tab

The Summarize options are just shortcuts or preconfigured Custom options such as reference Line, Band, and Distribution.

When using a Custom option, Tableau automatically opens a window to configure it. In this window, you can set the scope and the value, change the format, set the aggregation, and configure many other options. Here's an example of the **Add Reference Line**, **Band**, or **Box Plot** menu:

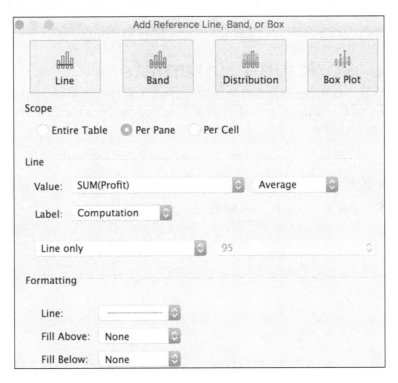

Another way to open this is with a right-click on an axis and by selecting **Add Reference Line**.

Custom options give you the liberty to choose precisely what you want to display. The available values when editing a reference Line, Band, or Box Plot are the pills in the View and the Parameters. You won't find all the Measures from the data source. If you want to build a reference Line, Band, or Box Plot with a specific Measure, you need to add it somewhere in the View (usually in the **Detail Mark** property, since it doesn't alter the visualization).

You can download the Analytics ZIP file from my website (`https://tableau2019.ladataviz.com`) in **Chapter 10: Analytics and Parameters**, or click on this direct link: `https://ladataviz.com/wp-content/uploads/2019/05/Analytics.zip`. When you unzip the file, you'll find a Tableau Package Workbook with an example of each Analytics option.

The last section of this chapter, *Creating a year-on-year comparator*, includes a concrete usage of a Custom Reference Line. But before that, we need to take a look at the last Tableau element, Parameters.

# How to work with Parameters

Parameters are a particular element in Tableau, such as Dimensions, Measures, and Sets. They can be Continuous or Discrete, depending on the data type in use. The two major aspects of Parameters are as follows:

- They are not linked to the data source (they don't rely on any field)
- They only return one value at a time

Let's start with how to create a Parameter.

# Creating a Parameter

To create a Parameter, you can use the small arrow next to **Dimensions**, as highlighted in the following screenshot:

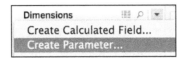

When you create a Parameter, Tableau automatically opens the **Edit Parameter** window, as illustrated in the following screenshot:

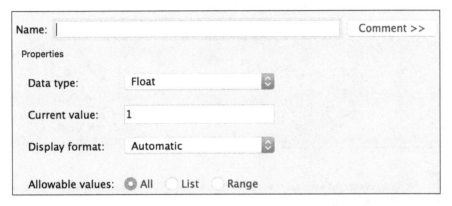

This window is the only place where you can configure a Parameter. At the top, you can specify its **Name** and add a **Comment** (visible when you hover over the field). You can also change the Parameter properties by defining the **Data type** and the **Current value** (the default value that the Parameter will have when you have created it). For some data types, you can also change the default **Display format**.

The last option, **Allowable values**, is a core element of a Parameter. As you know, a Parameter is not related to the dataset and can thereby take any possible value. With the **Allowable values** option, you can, however, limit the possibilities of what the users can enter. Let's spend some time learning a bit more about the three **Allowable values** options:

- The first option, **All**, allows all possible values to be entered.

- The second option, **List**, limits the values that a user can choose from a list. For each item, you can specify the value and the alias in the **Display As** column. You can enter the value manually, add all the values from a field, or paste copied values from your clipboard (from an Excel file, for example). Here's an example of the usage of **List**:

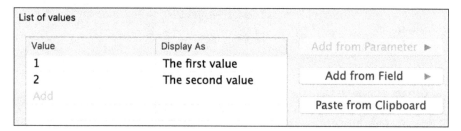

 You can add all the values from a field by right-clicking on it and using the **Create** option.

- The last option, **Range**, is available for Date, Date and Time, Integer, and Float. With Range, you can set a **Minimum**, a **Maximum**, and a **Step size**. The user will only be able to choose a value from that range. Here's an example of the usage of Range:

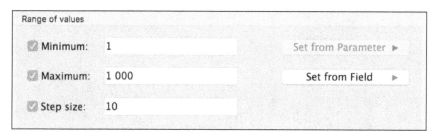

If you create a Boolean Parameter, you can't use those options, and you'll be limited to True and False. However, you can change the aliases.

Click on **OK**, and your Parameter will be ready! You may be wondering how you can use it. Continue reading!

# Using a Parameter

Usually, a Parameter is displayed on a Worksheet or a Dashboard. To display a Parameter on a Worksheet, right-click on it and select the **Show Parameter Control** option. On a Dashboard, you can add a Parameter from the options when you select a Worksheet or from the **Analysis** menu at the top.

 Since Tableau Desktop 2019.2, you can also update the value of a parameter with an Action, as shown in *Chapter 7, Powerful Dashboards, Stories, and Actions*.

Using the small arrow next to the parameter card, as highlighted in the following screenshot, you can change the display mode and find other options to customize:

Depending on the data type and the allowable value specified, the parameter can be displayed as follows:

- **As a Type In**, a free textbox where the users can enter any value they want
- **As a Slider**, which is usually associated with a ranged parameter
- **As a Compact List** or **Single Value List**, usually associated with a list parameter

So far, you've only learned how to create, configure, and display a Parameter. Displaying a Parameter and selecting a value has no impact. To use a Parameter, you need to put it in a Calculated Field.

The next section is a step-by-step tutorial where you'll see the potential of Parameters and how to use them to perform great analysis.

# Creating a year-on-year comparator

To create a year-on-year comparator, you need to combine everything that we have seen previously: **Calculated Field**, **Reference Line**, and **Parameter**.

Your mission (*if you accept it*) is to build a visualization where you can see the profit by region of a selected year compared to the previous year with a **Reference Line**. The **Color** also helps you to quickly spot the regions where the profit is lower than in the previous year. Here's the final result:

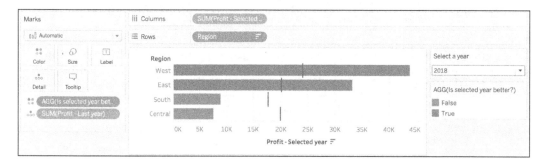

Quite impressive, isn't it? Let's build it! Follow this tutorial to learn how to do this:

1. Create a new Parameter and name it `Select a year`. Configure it as an **Integer** with a list of allowable values. The list is composed of four values: **2015**, **2016**, **2017**, and **2018**.

2. If you want to make it perfect, you can change the display of the values to remove the thousand.

3. Choose **2018** as the **Current value**.

   Your Parameter configuration window should look like this:

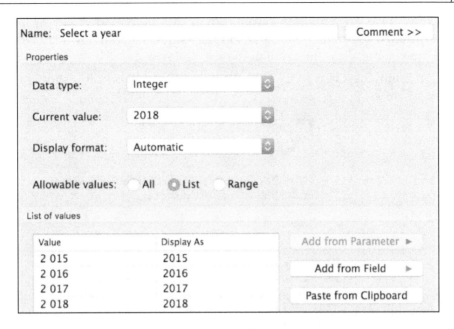

Name:  Select a year                                          Comment >>

Properties

Data type:        Integer

Current value:    2018

Display format:   Automatic

Allowable values:    All   ● List    Range

List of values

| Value | Display As | |
|---|---|---|
| 2 015 | 2015 | Add from Parameter ▸ |
| 2 016 | 2016 | Add from Field      ▸ |
| 2 017 | 2017 | |
| 2 018 | 2018 | Paste from Clipboard |

4.  Display your Parameter (right-click on it and select **Show Parameter Control**).

5.  Create a Calculated Field that will return the profit of the selected year. Name it `Profit - Selected year` and write the following formula inside it: `if YEAR([Order Date]) = [Select a year] then [Profit] END`. This formula returns the profit if the **Year of Order Date** is the same as the value of the parameter.

6.  Create a second Calculated Field, name it `Profit - Last year`, and write the following formula: `if YEAR([Order Date]) = [Select a year]-1 then [Profit] END`. This formula returns the profit if the **Year of Order Date** is the value of the Parameter minus one (so, if you select 2018 in the Parameter, the formula returns the profit value of 2017).

For each Calculated Field, make sure that the calculation is valid.

7. Now, you need to build the visualization. Put **Profit - Selected year** in **Columns**, **Region** in **Rows**, and sort the values. You can now play with the Parameter to show the Profit of the selected year.

8. Put **Profit - Last year** in the **Detail** property. Your Worksheet should look as follows:

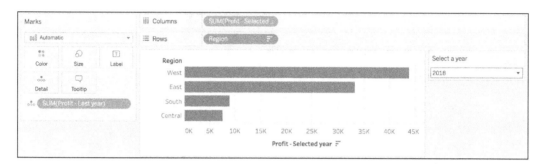

9. Go to the **Analytics** pane and add a **Custom Reference Line** in each cell. For the value of the reference **Line**, select **Profit - Last year** (the aggregation doesn't matter as we are on the cell level). In the **Formatting** section, you can make the line a bit darker. Here's how your reference **Line** should be configured:

10. Visually, you should be able the see the current and previous year's profit values, thanks to the reference Line.

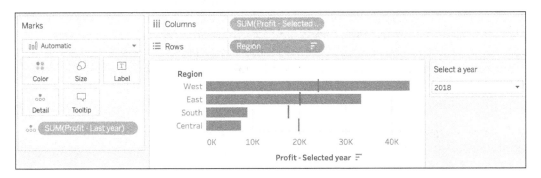

11. For a final touch, create a new Calculated Field, name it `Is selected year better?`, and write the following formula: `SUM([Profit - Selected year]) >= SUM([Profit - Last year])`. This Calculated Field returns `True` if the profit of the selected year is higher than the profit of the previous year and `False` if not.

12. Finally, put the new Calculated Field, **Is selected year better?**, in **Color**. If you want, you can modify the colors. In the end, your Worksheet should look as follows:

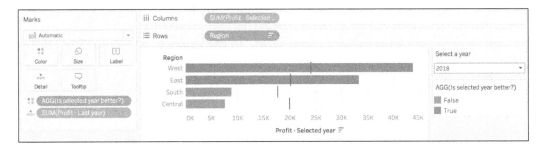

You can play with the Parameter to change the year, and you'll immediately spot the problematic region. This visualization is a good exercise because it makes you practice a lot of Tableau's features, and it's also a great way of comparing two different years.

# Summary

This chapter focused on two ways of enhancing your visualizations. With the Analytics tools, you can use models such as Trend Line, Cluster, and Forecast, but also all sorts of reference Lines, Bands, and Distribution. You can use all of these options to visualize your data in new ways and get a deeper understanding of it. With Parameters, you can create any input to interact with a visualization. The last section of this chapter summed up what you covered in this chapter with a real use case using Parameters and a reference Line.

In the next chapter, we'll talk about data sources again. You'll discover how to work with multiple data sources using a cross-database join and data blending, and how to create advanced unions.

# 11
# Advanced Data Connections

In a Workbook, you can add as many data sources as you want. In a Worksheet, you can see which data source is used thanks to the tick mark (✓) next to its icon, as shown in the following screenshot:

You can create different Worksheets based on different data sources and assemble them in a Dashboard. But what if you need more than that? What if you want to create a visualization using two different data sources, or create a unique data source based on a different type of connection? You can do all of that, too.

In this chapter about advanced data connections, we'll see how to work with multiple datasets, as well as some other new features for unions. The three sections of this chapter focus on the following:

- Cross-database join
- Data blending
- Wildcard union

The different examples require a specific dataset or file to be reproduced.

Let's start this chapter by learning how to combine multiple datasets in one data source.

# Cross-database join

In *Chapter 4*, *Connecting to Data and Simple Transformations*, you saw how to create joins between different tables of the same dataset. With cross-database joins, you can create joins between different tables from different connection types. It's a great way to add new dimensions to your analysis.

 You can't use all the different types of connections in a cross-database join.

As an example, let's create a join between Sample - Superstore and another Excel file, Reimbursement, which contains the reimbursed orders.

 To reproduce the following example, you need to download the Reimbursement Excel file available at https://tableau2019. ladataviz.com, in the **Chapter 11: Advanced Data Connections** section, or use this link: https://ladataviz.com/wp-content/ uploads/2018/09/Reimbursement.xlsx.

Here's what the Reimbursement table contains:

| Order ID | Reimbursed | Reason |
|---|---|---|
| CA-2015-115812 | y | Defect |
| CA-2017-152156 | y | Defect |
| CA-2017-111682 | y | Defect |
| CA-2017-145583 | y | Delay |
| CA-2017-130162 | n | New address |
| US-2017-123470 | y | Wrong product |

Let's see now how to create a cross-database join between those two files:

1. Open Tableau and click on the saved data source, Sample - Superstore.
2. Click on the **Data Source** tab at the bottom-left of the window to open the data source workplace.
3. Next to **Connections**, click on **Add** to connect to another file or server, as highlighted in the following screenshot:

4. Search and select the `Reimbursement` Excel file. Tableau automatically opens it in the same data source page, underneath `Sample - Superstore`.

5. Add the `Reimbursement` table as a left join on the `Order ID` column:

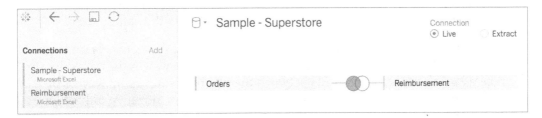

[  Each connection has a unique color, so it's easy to differentiate them. ]

6. In a new Worksheet, you can now create a visualization that combines the sales and the reason for reimbursement (exclude the null):

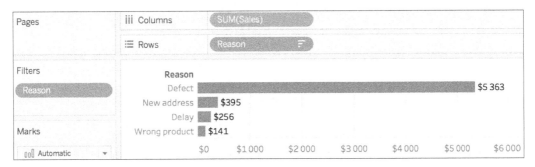

A cross-database join has the same disadvantage as a standard join: it can duplicate the data. However, it's a great feature that allows you to combine multiple datasets of different types in a unique data source.

The next section presents another way of combining two datasets.

# Data blending

Data blending is a way of using different fields from different data sources in one Worksheet. There is always a primary data source (the tick icon in blue) and one or more secondary data sources (the tick mark in orange). As for joins, one or multiple common fields are needed to create the relationships between the data sources.

Unlike joins, data blending is often used to add new Measures. Fields coming from the secondary data sources are always aggregated. However, they are only aggregated using the common fields between the two data sources, so there is no data duplication. However, data blending can rapidly have a negative impact on performance.

Fields with the same name can automatically be used to create a relationship. In the secondary data sources, you can recognize the fields that can be used for the relationship with the small *link* icon next to their name. You can click on the link icon to enable or disable them. For example, in the following screenshot, both **Order Date** and **Order Number** can be used as links, but only **Order Date** is selected and thus, used by Tableau:

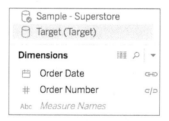

If no fields have the same name, you can use **Edit Relationships...** option from the **Data** top menu. A new window will open where you can configure the relationships, and, with the custom option, you can select the common fields manually. This will be illustrated in the following example.

[  If no fields are common, you can create a Calculated field to build the relationship. ]

Let's add a yearly target for our sales. In a previous chapter, we had to deduplicate the target value. You'll see that, with data blending, there is no need to do that.

 To reproduce the following example, you need to download the `Target` Excel file from `https://tableau2019.ladataviz.com`, in the **Chapter 11: Advanced Data Connections** section, or use this link: `https://ladataviz.com/wp-content/uploads/2018/09/Target.xlsx`.

Target is a simple Excel file with the Year and the value of the Target, as you can see here:

| Year | Target |
| --- | --- |
| 2015 | 500000 |
| 2016 | 500000 |
| 2017 | 500000 |
| 2018 | 700000 |

Go through the following steps to add a target to the sales:

1. Open Tableau Desktop and select the saved **Sample-Superstore** data source.
2. Click on the **New Data Source** icon in the toolbar: ⊟₊.
3. Search and select the `Target` Excel file that you've downloaded.
4. Click on **Sheet 1**; you should now have two different data sources, as shown in the following screenshot:

5. Create a bar chart with the year of the **Order Date** in **Columns** and the **Sales** in **Rows**.

6.  Add the **Target** Measure from the **Target** data source in **Detail**. A warning
    will open because Tableau isn't able to find a relationship between the two
    data sources. Your current visualization should look as follows:

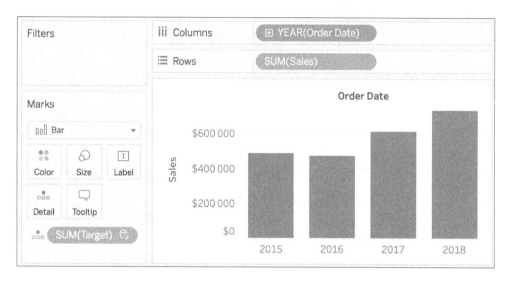

7.  Open the **Data** menu at the top and click on **Edit Relationships...**.

8.  Choose **Sample - Superstore** as the **Primary data source** and **Target** as the
    secondary, then select **Custom**. The configuration window should look
    as follows:

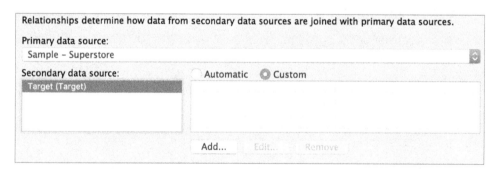

9. Click on the **Add...** button and, in the window that opens, select the **YEAR(Order Date)** field from the primary data source field and **Year** from the secondary, as highlighted in the following screenshot. Then click on **OK**:

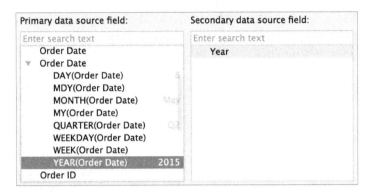

10. In the visualization, right-click on the axis and select **Add Reference Line**.

11. In the configuration window, change the scope to **Per Cell**, select **SUM(Target)** as the value, choose a **Custom** label, and write `Target`. Your configuration window and visualization should be similar to this screenshot:

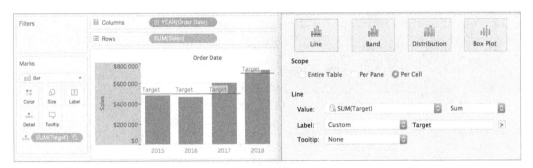

Adding the targets with a normal join will duplicate the values. Thanks to data blending, it's both easy and practical to add new Measures with different aggregations coming from different data sources. However, there are some limitations, such as you can't use the count distinct or median aggregation, and **Level of Detail (LOD)** calculations are not allowed.

In the next section, unions are back!

# Wildcard union

The first time you saw how to create unions, you had to select the different tables of the dataset that you wanted to use manually. Wildcard unions allow you to create more powerful unions that automatically add all the files and all the tables that match a specific pattern. This kind of union is convenient because you don't have to add the new tables manually; you only need to refresh the data source.

As an example of a wildcard union, I am going to split the `Sample-Superstore` Excel file into four Excel files, one for each year, and put them in a folder named `Sales`.

 To reproduce the following example, you need to download the `Sales.zip` file from `https://tableau2019.ladataviz.com`, in the **Chapter 11: Advanced Data Connections** section, or use this link: `https://ladataviz.com/wp-content/uploads/2018/09/Sales.zip`.

Let's union those files:

1. First, unzip the `Sales.zip` file you've just downloaded.
2. Open Tableau Desktop and chose **Microsoft Excel** from the list of connectors.
3. Navigate to the `Sales` unzipped folder and select the `Sales 2015.xlsx` file.
4. Replace **Sheet1** with **New Union**:

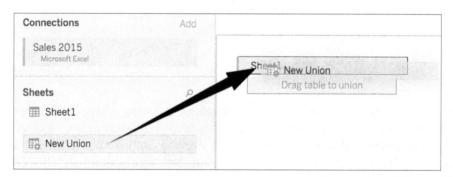

5. Select the second tab, **Wildcard**, and configure it to include all the sheets named `Sheet1`, and all the Excel Workbooks starting with *Sales* by writing `Sales *.xlsx` (use the * symbol to represent any other characters).

Your configuration window should look like this:

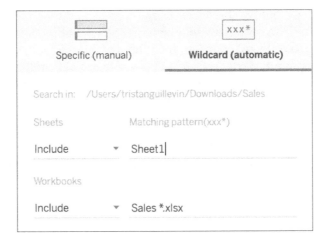

 You can also expand the search to the subfolders or parent folders using the options.

6. That's it! To test the wildcard union, you can create a new visualization that displays the **Year of Order Date** and the **Sales**, with the **Path** of the different files:

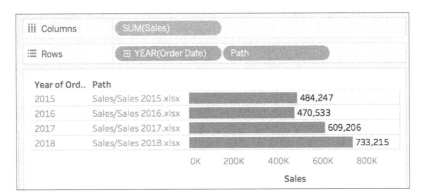

Wildcard unions are very practical. Use them as often as you can! The only rule is to be careful with the patterns so that you don't include things you don't want!

# Summary

This chapter was short, but the three new features presented will undoubtedly be useful for you! With a cross-database join, you can create a unique data sources that combine multiple different connections. With data blending, you can create a relationship between multiple data sources and use their fields in the same Worksheet. Finally, you learned how to give superpowers to unions thanks to wildcard unions, a feature that automatically adds files and tables based on a pattern.

We have one last technical chapter to go, and it's not a trivial one, since we'll be talking about security. You will see how to secure your data on Tableau Server and in Tableau Desktop, thanks to three different layers of protection. What are you waiting for? You're almost at the end!

# 12
# Dealing with Security

In this last advanced chapter, we'll speak about security, which is an essential aspect of working with data. To add protection, you need to have Tableau Server. In this chapter, we'll focus on three ways of dealing with security, including the following:

- Tableau Server security
- User filters
- Row-level filters

To manage security on Tableau Server, you need to have sufficient privileges on it. To add the user filter and build the Row-level security filter, you need at least one a way to connect to Tableau Server. Let's start with the most straightforward way of securing your data on Tableau Server.

## Tableau Server security

To protect your Tableau Server contents, you can click on the three dots, **...**, on any content (project, workbooks, views, and Flows) to show the options and select **Permissions**. When you click on **Permissions**, Tableau opens a new window where you can specify many security options.

Here's the **Permissions** menu:

On this menu, you'll always see the **All Users** permissions. You can click on the three dots to edit them. You can also click on **Add a user or group rule** to specify new permissions for specific users or groups. When you edit the permissions, you can see, for each element, a list of preconfigured roles.

If you click on the arrows next to an element (Project, Workbooks, Data Sources, and flows), you get more detail and the possibility to edit each permission individually. Each permission can be allowed (green), denied (red), or unspecified (grey). To edit an individual permission, click on its box.

Here's an example of permissions with a detailed view for Workbooks:

Be aware that not all options are available for all elements. Here's the complete list of permissions, grouped by the elements where they appear:

- **Global permissions**:
    - **View** 👁 : Specifies whether a user can see the element
    - **Save** 🖫 : Overwrites the existing element on the server

- **Project permissions**:
    - **Project leader** 👤: A project leader has all the permissions on that project.

- **Workbook, Data Sources, and Flows Permissions**:
    - **Download** ⬇/⬆: Downloads the file
    - **Delete** 🗑: Removes the element from the server
    - **Set Permissions** ✅: Gives us the ability to change and define the permissions
    - **Move** 📁: Changes the project of a Workbook or Flow
    - **Connect/Run** 🔗 : Gives us the ability to connect to the Data Source or run Tableau Prep Flow

- **Workbook Permissions**:
    - **Download image** 📈: Downloads an image of the visualization
    - **Download summary data** ≣ : Downloads a summary of the data in a visualization
    - **View comments** 💬: Sees the comments posted under a visualization
    - **Add comments** 💬+: Adds comments under a visualization
    - **Filter** ▽ : Uses the filters available and the **Keep Only** and **Exclude** features
    - **Download full data** ▥ : Downloads the complete data used in a visualization, with all the rows and columns
    - **Share customized** 📊: Gives us the ability to create and share a customized view
    - **Web edit** ✏ : Opens the Tableau Server edition window where a user can modify the visualization or create new ones

With those permissions, you can control who has access to what on Tableau Server. You can, for example, allow only a few users to access your Workbook. But what if you want to control what those users can see?

# User filters

Let's say that, based on the `Sample - Superstore` data source, you want to control the Region that the users can see. To do that, you need to set a **User Filter**.

User filters are a special kind set on Tableau Desktop. They link Tableau Server users to dimension values. It's quite easy to create a user filter:

1. On Tableau Desktop, click on the **Server** in the top menu, go to **Create a User Filter**, and choose the Field to secure.

2. Tableau opens a new window where you can select, on the left, a **User** or a **Group** and, on the right, the **Members** of the field that the user or group can see.

3. Once you've created the user filter, you'll see a new set in your data source.

4. To use a user filter, add the corresponding set to the **Filter** shelf or, better, as a Data Source Filter (with the **Use all** option).

The reason it's better to add a **User Filter** on the Data Source filters rather than the **Filter** shelf is to increase security. If you put a User Filter in the Filter shelf, a user may be able to download the Workbook and remove the User Filter from the Filters. They'll have access to all the data. Also, if someone starts a new analysis based on this Data Source, they'll also have access to all the data. If you put the User Filter on the Data Source Filters, the users won't be able to remove it without having the right to edit a Data Source, and it will be automatically applied when using this Data Source.

Now, to illustrate the usage of a User Filter, let's look at an example with the `Sample - Superstore` Data Source. For this example, I've created five groups on Tableau Server: `Central Users`, `South Users`, `West Users`, `East Users`, and `Top Management`.

It's not a problem if you can't create the same groups as me to replicate this example. Just use existing **groups** or **users** on your Tableau Server; you can't break anything.

Let's start creating User Filters:

1. Create a new **User Filter** on **Region...** and name it `Region Filter`:

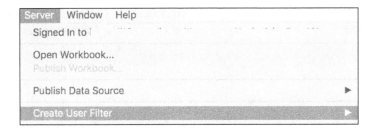

2.  In the **User Filter** configuration window, for each group, select the members of the field that they are allowed to see. For example, click on the **West Users** group and select the **West** value. For the **Top Management** group, select **All members**, and for **All Users**, select **None**. Here's an example of the configuration for the **West Users** group:

3.  Build a simple visualization: double-click on **State** and then add **Sales** on **Color**.

4.  Put the **Region Filter** set in the **Filter** shelf to test it. If you're not inside one of the groups where we define access, you shouldn't see anything.

5.  At the very bottom of the Tableau window, you can see the currently logged-in user in Tableau Server, as shown in the following screenshot:

6.  Beside the name of the logged-in user, there's an arrow you can click on to select another User or Group.

7.  With this option, choose the **West** group, and the User Filter will automatically filter the Region to keep only the **West** value, as you can see here:

8.  You can test the same with **Top Management** — all the regions will be displayed. When you're confident that the User Filter works fine, you can remove it from the **Filters** shelf.

9.  Right-click on the Data Source name and select **Edit Data Source Filters**.

10. Click on the **Add** button and select **Region Filter** field.

11. Select the **Use all** option and click on **OK**. The User Filter is applied on all the Data Source, thereby enhancing the security of your data.

This is the first way of securing your data. As you may have guessed, if you have hundreds of users to give access to, and hundreds of different values in the field to secure, the User Filter will be extremely long to create and impossible to maintain. In those cases, we create a row-level filter.

# Row-level filters

To create a row-lever filter, your Data Source must contain a field with the name of the Tableau Server Users. This solution only works when the access level is already defined in your data. This option uses a Tableau function called USERNAME() that returns the username of the currently logged-in user.

Again, the best way to understand this is with an example. You can reproduce the tutorial with your own Users and Groups in your Tableau Server and the Sample - Superstore Data Source.

In my case, I've created three Users in Tableau Server and the following Excel file, which I named User Access.xlsx:

| Region | User |
|--------|------|
| Central | johnsnow@example.com |
| West | johnsnow@example.com |
| East | johnsnow@example.com |
| South | johnsnow@example.com |
| West | williamplayfair@example.com |
| Central | charlesminard@example.com |

In the Excel file, we specified that the following:

- *John Snow* has access to all the Regions (*do not confuse John Snow, a famous epidemiologist who discovered, in 1854, that cholera deaths were clustered around the water pumps in London thanks to data visualization, with Jon Snow, who knows nothing*).

- *William Playfair* only has access to *West*.

- *Charles Minard* only has access to *Central*.

Here's the step-by-step guide of how to create a row-level filter between the data and Tableau Server:

1.  Open Tableau and connect to the `Sample - Superstore` Excel file.

2.  Add another Microsoft new Excel connection to the **User Access** file.

3.  Create a cross-database join between **Orders** and **User Access** on the common **Region** field:

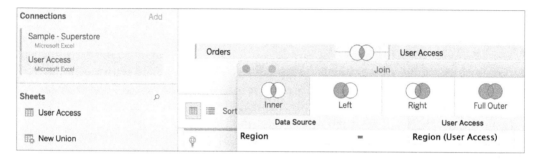

 This join duplicates the data by the number of users, but since you never show multiple users at the same time, it's not a problem.

4.  On a Worksheet, create a new calculated field, name it `User has access`, and write `USERNAME() = [User]`. This calculation returns `True` if the currently logged-in user is the same as the **User** field in the data source.

5.  Right-click on the data source name and select **Edit Data Source Filters**. Add the **User has access** Calculated Field and keep only the value, that is, **True**. The data source filter should look as follows:

6. You can test the row-level filter by selecting different users on Tableau Server with the bottom menu. Here is, for example, the result for **Charles Minard**, who only has access to the **Central** regions:

 Before Tableau 2018.3, the only drawback was data duplication: when using an extract, all the duplicated lines must be generated, which makes the extract gigantic. Since Tableau 2018.3, you can use the multiple table schema when creating an extract with joins. This drastically decreases the extract size when using a row-level filter.

With this solution, you let the data control the security. It's a great way to handle complex situations because you can create row-level filters based on multiple fields.

# Summary

In this last technical chapter, you learned how to secure your data and content on Tableau Server. The permissions allow you to control who can see your work and what power they have over it (such as to download, save, edit, and more). On Tableau Desktop, with user filters and row-level filters, you can control what the users can see in your data.

This book is almost finished. We've covered all the technical aspects of Tableau. The last chapter is an invitation for you to join the Tableau Community, along with tips on how to get better and better each day with different community projects.

# Section 4: After Finishing the Book

It's almost time to say goodbye and close this book. This conclusion is more an opening than an ending. You'll see all the options available to continue your journey with Tableau keep growing your skills.

This section includes the following chapter:

- *Chapter 13, How to Keep Growing your Skills*

# 13
# How to Keep
# Growing Your Skills

That's it! You are now all set to use Tableau in a professional environment, starting with connecting to your data, building your data source, then your first visualizations and Dashboards, after which you publish all your work in a secure and online environment. But there is still a lot to discover and many ways to become better at using Tableau.

In this short chapter, we'll speak about the following:

- The Tableau Community
- Tableau Public
- Community projects
- Ambassadors, Zen Masters, and Iron Viz

Let's start with the reason Tableau is the best tool for data visualization: the Community.

## The Tableau Community

Tableau is an excellent tool for many reasons, but there are a lot of great tools for data visualization. If you ask me why Tableau is better than the others, my answer would be, *the Community*.

When I started using Tableau, the Tableau Community Forums helped me a lot. No questions are left unanswered, and you'll find a lot of people that are eager to help you. Don't hesitate to ask any questions here: `https://community.tableau.com/community/forums`.

The community is all about sharing. There are many events where the Tableau Community gathers to share. The **Tableau User Group** (TUG) is a regional event (check whether there's one near your area!) where senior users meet new users and discuss new features, tips, use cases, and more. It's also a great place to share pizzas and beers!

Don't be sad if there is no TUG near you; there are many online events, such as the Fringe Festival, that are organized by the Tableau community: `http://www.thefringefestival.rocks/`.

Of course, there are also two major official events: the Tableau Conference in the US and the European Tableau Conference in Europe. These are the biggest Tableau events, and they are the best places to meet people, discover all the new features to be released, and cheer on your favorite competitor at the Iron Viz event.

You'll find all the events, groups, forums, links, and webinars here: `https://www.tableau.com/Community`.

The other great way to learn is on Tableau Public.

# Tableau Public

Tableau Public is a piece of software, similar to Tableau Desktop, that you can download and use for free with some limitations: you need to publish your work online in a public environment, and you don't have access to all the connectors that are available in Tableau Desktop.

Tableau Public is, in fact, much more than that.

Tableau Public is like a social network where you can only find the best visualizations available. As we are data lovers, here are some figures: 250,000 Tableau Public users have published more than 1 million Workbooks, generating more than 1 billion views.

On the Tableau Public website, you can find a **Viz Of The Day** section on the home page (every day, a new Workbook is promoted by Tableau: `https://public.tableau.com/en-us/s/`), and many featured visualizations in different categories (Greatest Hits, Sports, Social Goof, and so on). You can find a list of the current featured authors, a blog, and many resources to keep learning. You can also search for any author or interest. But wait – the best is yet to come.

At the bottom of every visualization published in Tableau Public, there are some buttons to open the visualization in full screen, share, and the best: download. When you click on the download button, you can get an image, the data, a crosstab, a PDF, and – *are you ready?* – the Workbook itself! Even the most beautiful Workbooks can usually be downloaded (it's the author's choice). It is one of the greatest ways to learn. I discover a lot by downloading the Workbooks and figuring out how the authors built them.

Creating a Tableau Public account is very simple. Once you have an account, you can start to follow authors you like and publish Workbooks.

The main reason why people don't share Workbooks in Tableau Public is that they don't know what data to share. The next section resolves that problem.

# Community projects

This section is all about growing your Tableau skills. There are many projects being created by the community for the Community. Participating in those projects doesn't engage you in anything; you can only learn and become better. For the majority of those projects, people interact through Twitter, so I advise you to create an account to follow those projects.

Here are some Community projects:

- **Viz For Social Good – #VizForSocialGood** by *Chloe Tseng*: This project gives you the opportunity to work for non-profit organizations such as UNICEF and the United Nations. There is a new project almost every month, with a deadline to respect. You can register as a volunteer to be informed of new projects. At the end of every project, the non-profit organization chooses one visualization to feature on its communication channels.

  Viz For Social Good was awarded a Silver for Community at the 2017 Information is Beautiful Awards.

 All the information that is required so that you can join can be found here: https://www.vizforsocialgood.com.

- **Make Over Monday – #MakeOverMonday**—by *Eva Murray* and *Andy Kriebel*: This is probably the most followed project and the best way to practice your creativity in Tableau. Every Monday, they share a new dataset to visualize in Tableau. On Wednesday, there is a webinar where Eva and Andy review some visualizations (*#MMVizReview*) and, during the weekend, they publish a blog post with all the lessons they've learned and their favorite makeovers.

You'll find all the information about this, datasets, and links here: `https://www.makeovermonday.co.uk/`.

- **Workout Wednesday – #WorkOutWednesday**—currently run by *Luke Stanke, Ann Jackson, Curtis Harris, Lorna Eden*, and guests: This is the most challenging Community project. Every Wednesday, they share a new visualization and the dataset that's required to reproduce it. The goal is to rebuild the same visualization. Of course, it's more difficult than you think. If **Make Over Monday** helps you practice your creativity, **Workout Wednesday** is all about technical challenges.

Find all the challenges at `http://www.workout-wednesday.com/weekly-overview/`.

There are other projects, such as **Data For a Cause** (*#DataForACause*) (`www.olgatsubiks.com/data-for-a-cause`) by Olga Tsubiks, and **Sports Viz Sunday** (*#SportsVizSunday*) (`https://data.world/sportsvizsunday`) by Simon Beaumont and Spencer Baucke, that I invite you to follow.

As you can see, there are many ways to learn and become better at using Tableau. Maybe, after some time, you'll compete as an Iron Viz contestant, or you'll be recognized as one of the Ambassadors or Zen Masters. Don't know what I'm talking about? The next – and last – section explains everything.

# Ambassadors, Zen Masters, and Iron Viz

When you start in the Tableau Community, it may be hard to know who to follow. Tableau has decided to help you by recognizing the investment and spirit of some people in the Community.

## Ambassadors

The first set of amazing people are the Ambassadors. They are split into four groups:

- **Forums Ambassadors:** They are there to answer your questions in the Forum.
- **Social Media Ambassadors:** They are the social network gurus; follow them to get all the latest news.
- **User Group Leader Ambassadors:** They help the Community meet in real life by organizing Tableau User Groups .
- **Tableau Public Ambassadors:** Check their Tableau Public profiles and be ready to be blown away.

You can find all the current **Ambassadors** here: `https://www.tableau.com/ tableau-ambassadors`.

## Zen Masters

The second set of amazing people is the **Zen Masters**. They are the faces of Tableau Community. They passionately dedicate a huge amount of time to help everyone excel in Tableau. They not only create great visualizations, but they also share their knowledge as much as they can. Everyone in the Tableau Community has learned at least one thing from a **Zen Master**.

Discover who the **Zen Masters** are and what they are doing at `https://www.tableau.com/zen-masters`.

## Iron Viz

As you enhance your skills, you may want to try to compete against other people in the Community. For that, you have Iron Viz. The competition is divided into two parts: three qualification contests, called the Feeders, and one Final. For the Feeders, only the theme is imposed, and the contestants have approximately one month to find the data and create the best possible visualization. There is one winner per Feeder.

The three winners of the Feeders battle during the Iron Viz Final at the annual Tableau Conference. There is no way to prepare for the Final: build a Workbook from the start, in 20 minutes, live, in front of thousands of screaming people. A jury, composed of four people, and the public, vote on Twitter to determine the annual Iron Viz champion. Since 2017, there is also a European Iron Viz competition. All the information about the Iron Viz competition are available here: `https://www.tableau.com/iron-viz`.

I advise you to participate – not for the purpose of winning, but to push yourself further than you've ever gone in Tableau. You cannot lose; either you win, or you learn.

# Summary

This chapter, even though it's not technical, is really important. This chapter is the key to continuing your journey with Tableau. This chapter is also my tribute to the Community, who kept pushing me higher and higher over the last three years since I started using Tableau.

Even if you don't plan on sharing a lot or getting involved (which is understandable), keep in mind that the Community Forum is the first place to go if you have any questions regarding Tableau. Even though I tried my best to explain all the concepts in this book, no books or training sessions can cover every use case you will encounter in real life. Also, if you're searching for resources, blogs, inspiration, or webinars, you'll find it on Tableau Public or through the Community Projects.

Thanks for purchasing and reading this book. I truly hope that you've learned a lot and that you'll use Tableau with the same passion I do.

# Other Books You May Enjoy

If you enjoyed this book, you may be interested in another book by Packt:

**Tableau 2019.x Cookbook**

Dmitry Anoshin, Teodora Matic, Et al

ISBN: 978-1-78953-338-5

- ▸ Understand the basic and advanced skills of Tableau Desktop
- ▸ Implement best practices of visualization, dashboard, and storytelling
- ▸ Learn advanced analytics with the use of build in statistics
- ▸ Deploy the multi-node server on Linux and Windows
- ▸ Use Tableau with big data sources such as Hadoop, Athena, and Spectrum
- ▸ Cover Tableau built-in functions for forecasting using R packages
- ▸ Combine, shape, and clean data for analysis using Tableau Prep
- ▸ Extend Tableau's functionalities with REST API and R/Python

**Tableau 2019.1 for Data Scientists [Video]**

Manja Bogicevic

ISBN: 978-1-78995-824-9

- ▸ Connect Tableau to various datasets and gather data from sources such as Excel and CSV files
- ▸ Work with full-suite visuals and create bar charts, area charts, maps and scatterplots, and treemaps and pie charts
- ▸ Explore storytelling and how to choose the best colors for your dashboards
- ▸ Discover the types of joins and how they work
- ▸ Work with data blending in Tableau
- ▸ Export results from Tableau into PowerPoint, Word, and other software
- ▸ Understand aggregation, granularity, and level of detail
- ▸ Study advanced data preparation in Tableau and profit analysis

# Leave a review – let other readers know what you think

Please share your thoughts on this book with others by leaving a review on the site that you bought it from. If you purchased the book from Amazon, please leave us an honest review on this book's Amazon page. This is vital so that other potential readers can see and use your unbiased opinion to make purchasing decisions, we can understand what our customers think about our products, and our authors can see your feedback on the title that they have worked with Packt to create. It will only take a few minutes of your time, but is valuable to other potential customers, our authors, and Packt. Thank you!

# Index

CPSIA information can be obtained
at www.ICGtesting.com
Printed in the USA
LVHW061609310720
662091LV00007B/320

9 781838 553067